The
VALLEYS

The VALLEYS

Edited by
John Davies &
Mike Jenkins

POETRY WALES PRESS
1984

PUBLISHED IN 1984 BY POETRY WALES PRESS
56 PARCAU AVENUE, BRIDGEND, MID GLAMORGAN

British Library Cataloguing in Publication Data

The Valleys.
  1. English literature   2. Glamorgan—
Literary collections   3. Gwent—Literary
collections
I. Davies, John, *1944*—   II. Jenkins, Mike, *1953*—
820.8'0324294   PR1111.G5/

ISBN 0-907476-31-7
ISBN 0-907476-28-7

Cover Design: Cloud 9 Design
Cover Painting: 'Glyncorrwg' by David Carpanini

The publisher gratefully acknowledges the financial assistance
of the Welsh Arts Council

PRINTED IN 10pt BASKERVILLE
BY
BRIDGEND PRINTING COMPANY LTD.,
TREMAINS ROAD, BRIDGEND, MID GLAMORGAN.

Contents

Illustrations

Foreword

The Valleys has been a long time coming: hitherto there has been no anthology of poetry or prose from the industrial valleys of South Wales. Both within Wales and beyond, consciousness of the area has been strongly influenced by its most powerful literary voice, Richard Llewellyn's in *How Green Was My Valley*. That novel's glamorisation of the rural past, its sentimental stereo-typing of people and caricature of life generally in the Valleys, are mists which linger still. Not that, in literary terms, sharp documentary realism alone is valid. It has been our intention to present a variety of styles and approaches with the reader's enjoyment in mind — particularly readers in or originally from the Valleys. Our hope is that they will recognise and relish as versions of reality the poems, short stories and excerpts from novels included here.

To an even greater extent than Welsh literature in English generally, the writing of this area has reflected the lives of working people. Invariably it has shared their political aspirations of socialism and communism although, since the emergence of poets like Harri Webb during the nineteen-sixties, it has embodied a nationalistic spirit unrepresentative of the majority. Whether or not this is a prophetic spirit remains to be seen. What is certain, however, is that the writing of the Valleys has reached few people in the area itself let alone beyond it. The reasons for this are many, though the influence of London-centred mass media and of a basically middle-class education system are two key factors. It is sad that few children in the Rhondda will leave school having heard of Idris Davies or Gwyn Thomas, that fewer still will have been introduced to their poems and stories.

More than anything else it was coal that established the Valleys as an entity. But the development of the iron industry between about 1760 and 1850 preceded that of coal, and the capital of iron was Merthyr Tydfil. Later, Jack Jones was to write prodigiously about this town, seeming to have every required fact stored in his squirrel's drey of a mind. Iron acted like a magnet on people. From rural Wales they came, from Ireland and Spain, yet many ended up living in misery in town slums where poverty, disease and crime were endemic. Some time later in the nineteenth century, when steam power was applied to transport in the form of railways and steam ships, there came a huge and worldwide demand for steam coal. And, by the nineteen-twenties and thirties, the Valleys' dependence on coal was almost total during a period which saw the first upsurge of prose and poetry, a time of ferment and drama. Coal-mining made for hardship. Yet it also forged close-knit communities and a new political awareness which culminated in the Welsh miners' determined stand during the General Strike of 1926. Tensions between a new, challenging Marxism and the traditional religious nonconformity were at their height then. Amongst others, D. Gwenallt Jones in Welsh and Idris Davies in English evoked these tensions in their poetry, celebrating at the same time the unsung heroism of the miners and their families during the Depression of the 1930s. Many felt forced to leave for London and the Midlands in search of work. After the massive influx of miners and their families between 1850 and 1910, a short period of relative stability ended with the emigration of some four hundred thousand people between 1920 and 1930. It was a decline akin to that of more recent times (the population of the Rhondda fell by twenty per cent between 1951 and 1971) but intensified by terrible poverty, by the struggle for life's basics of food and clothing.

Since the nineteen-thirties, the Valleys have experienced some prosperity and then rapid decay. During the nineteen-sixties alone, an average of ten pits closed each year and now the Valleys share the visible marks of dereliction. The decay in political radicalism sketched in Tom Earley's poem 'Rebel's Progress' has altered literary perspectives but hasn't, however, sapped literary vitality: in their different ways Ron Berry, Alun Richards and John L. Hughes all reflect the defiant humour of the people in an ironic, cool-eyed prose very different from the ideological intensity of many writers of the thirties.

The anthology's structure reflects the modern period of this historical outline with its hills and valleys of upsurge and decline. A thematic approach would have led inevitably, we felt, to the inclusion of some items simply because they happened to fit the category of chapel, sport, mine or whatever — and to the rejection of worthwhile material which didn't. As

8

it is, our main criticism for inclusion has been literary quality. Any anthology, though, will make on its editors those demands of balance and variety which both complicate and enrich the process of selection. And ultimately, of course, our aim was to reflect the reality of a unique place and the spirit of its people through words that survive and vibrate as strongly as that spirit.

John Davies
Mike Jenkins

The Collier

Vernon Watkins

When I was born on Amman hill
A dark bird crossed the sun.
Sharp on the floor the shadow fell;
I was the youngest son.

And when I went to the County School
I worked in a shaft of light.
In the wood of the desk I cut my name:
Dai for Dynamite.

The tall black hills my brothers stood;
Their lessons all were done.
From the door of the school when I ran out
They frowned to watch me run.

The slow grey bells they rung a chime
Surly with grief or age.
Clever or clumsy, lad or lout,
All would look for a wage.

I learnt the valley flowers' names
And the rough bark knew my knees.
I brought home trout from the river
And spotted eggs from the trees.

A coloured coat I was given to wear
Where the lights of the rough land shone.
Still jealous of my favour
The tall black hills looked on.

They dipped my coat in the blood of a kid
And they cast me down a pit,
And although I crossed with strangers
There was no way up from it.

11

Soon as I went from the County School
I worked in a shaft. Said Jim,
'You will get your chain of gold, my lad,
But not for a likely time.'

And one said, 'Jack was not raised up
When the wind blew out the light
Though he interpreted their dreams
And guessed their fears by night.'

And Tom, he shivered his leper's lamp
For the stain that round him grew;
And I heard mouths pray in the after-damp
When the picks would not break through.

They changed words there in darkness
And still through my head they run,
And white on my limbs is the linen sheet
And gold on my neck the sun.

from Bidden to the Feast

Jack Jones

(Published in 1938, Jack Jones' novel is set in his home town of Merthyr Tydfil in the late nineteenth century. At its centre is Megan Davies who began work in a brickyard at the age of ten and who assumes responsibility for the family after her mother's death. Jack Jones offers the reader detailed insights into the history and character of Merthyr; in this extract, he evokes the threat represented by cholera early in the century.)

A theatre for a season, and circuses here to-day and gone to-morrow, had previously occupied the site which the most popular of all Cheap Jack's had now been occupying for months past. Already he was the talk not only of Merthyr and Dowlais, but also of the district for miles around, and on pay-Saturdays people came over the mountains from other valleys with gold and silver money to spend at his place, for wasn't he a universal provider. 'You can get anything an' everything at the Cheap Jack's — 'cept beer, of course, for he haven't got a licence,' the people said. . . .

Yes, the Cheap Jack had a cure for the old Cholera which came every now and then to take hundreds of people to their graves out of the way. There was no end to the cures for the old Cholera. Druggists sold powders to cure it, old women compounded herbs to cure one of it, many who had never been to chapel before ran to chapel when the old Cholera was about, and the Cheap Jack he sold the lozenges which he said wouldn't hurt one if so be that it didn't cure. More a preventative to render one immune than a cure once it got hold of you, was what he maintained, so he sold tons of those lozenges which the people chewed and chewed whilst the sale went on. Those in the district who were members of the Latter-Day Saints had their own secret way of dealing with the old Cholera when it came, but their way of dealing with it was reserved for members only. But as most of the people stricken by the old Cholera were far from being saints, latter-day or any day at all, the cure in the custody of the Latter-Day Saints of the district was not available to them. The doctors warned the people against all the quack remedies they went after when the old Cholera was about. Powders, herbs, lozenges were no good, the doctors said. Cleanliness, they talked about. Said that the graveyards crammed with dead above the level of the houses in which people alive were living atop of each other — Of course, most of our chapels had their graveyards, in front of the chapels some of them were, others were at the back. Not much bigger than a couple of full-sized blankets some of the chapel graveyards, and hundreds if not thousands buried in 'em. Now, of course, with the Cefn Cemetery opened, the doctors didn't have the chapel graveyards, many of them side of the road and in the middle and above houses, to talk about. So they talked about our privies over cesspools, irregular and inadequate supply of water, pigsties and stables and ash-heaps and stagnant pools and casks for pigs' wash stinking in front of houses, and all this in such a big place so overcrowded, the doctors said. . . .

Well, perhaps there was something in what the doctors said, for it was a big district — the fact that it had to have two Members of Parliament proves that it was a big district. Then look at the number there was working in Merthyr and Dowlais. In the Guest works and pits of Dowlais employment was provided for seven thousand five hundred men, women and children. The Cyfarthfa works and pits owned by Mr. Crawshay provided employment for another six thousand men, women and children, and the Plymouth pits provided employment for several thousand men, women and children. Then the brickyards, foundries and factories an' shops an' things provided employment for thousands more, so it must have been a big district. A stranger standing on the mountain looking down would never believe that so many people lived in so few homes. But they did and the living were more crowded in their houses than the dead were in the chapel graveyards. Those who had passed away within the last five years had twenty-one acres of as lovely country as anyone could wish to be put to lie in. Up above the Cefn under the trees in which the birds sang all the day long, up there where everything was so clean, sweet and lovely, they were taking the dead out of the sight of the works and pits many of them had been worked to death and done to death in. The living remained badly-housed under the shadow of Cholera, and the doctors who were all Company doctors swore under their breath when visiting Cholera cases in Company houses. Everything was Company-owned and controlled. Schools, houses, doctors, teachers, clergymen of the Church of England, canal, railways, banks, souls. So the Company doctors didn't dare open their mouths too wide about the housing conditions of the place.

From hovels strong hairy-chested breadwinners went to their work in the morning without as much as a pain in the belly, to return dying from Cholera in the evening — so no wonder the people in the Cheap Jack's chewed his Cholera lozenges. Twenty-four hours was all the Cholera required to bring down the strong to the graves — the stronger they were the better the Cholera liked 'em. Diarrhoea — and the men from the furnaces, men from the rolls, men down the pits, men everywhere running like mad to open their trousers time and again. Crawling home with cramps in the limbs — "What in the name o' God is the matter with you, my John, my Tom, my Dick, my Harry?" Cold — clammy — "O-o-o-o-oh, run for the doctor," who when he comes can only shake his head. Sound the alarm along the stinking brook and river banked both sides with houses crowded. The timid with no more than a touch of bellyache crying in the night: "It's got me, the old Cholera's got me." Stricken houses — "keep away from them. But I must go an' see my mother. Awa-a-a-ay for your life." Doctors on their rounds not fearing, here and there a doctor having to pay the price. Brave Brodie and other doctors without sleep for many nights put to sleep for ever an' greater love hath no man. . . . Men whose cramped limbs slow them down clinging to the iron standards of gas-lamps avoided — "only Thou, O God." Mother of nine with her shawl over her head twtting down quiet in one of the Tramroad's dark stretches, the people hurrying by — "only Thou, O God." A brickyard gel on her way home from work with the other gels puts her hands to her stomach and moans: "I must go somewhere again," she trots like the drunken in one direction, the other gels flee her the other — "only Thou, O God."

Before it spends itself the old Cholera strikes two thousand this time again. Doctors with the help of God manage to save nearly seventeen hundred souls alive. Two hundred, which is ten per cent of two thousand, are taken quickly, the other hundred die of the complications, chief of which is fatal Uremia. Rails Russia wants more and more of, so we'll have to get more hands from somewhere to replace those taken by the Cholera. Irish from Ireland, Cornishmen from Cornwall, Staffordshire men from Staffordshire, men from everywhere are invited to come and share our great prosperity, to earn good wages — "an' bring your families with you." They come to stoke our furnaces, to roll our rails, to hew our coal, to live two families in one house, to keep beds warm all the year round by the system of shift-sleeping — and here are many of them chewing Cholera lozenges in the Cheap Jack's on towards the end of another dry summer. They are uneasy, for this is the kind o' weather when the old Cholera might visit 'em again — p'raps it's not gone from here. Sure to be though, for they have heard talk that it is over in Tredegar now, and most of them believed that the old Cholera, like a man, could not be in two places same time. Ninety-nine of every hundred now assembled at the Cheap Jack's are of that belief.

from Rubaiyat

Roy Burnett

God made the world in 1929.
Original winds beat at a cottage door,
Snow on the streets, the hills, and every sign
Opaque with ice. No winter was before
Nor summer overseas, but life was mine
Enshawled with love amongst the valley's poor.

It's said (I say) that memory must forget
The hunch-backed darkness, comfort of the womb,
The milky sex of suckling blood, and yet
I draw a picture of a lamplit room
From harbouring thighs. Without a word I get
The picture's name. I know the word was home.

So I remember clouds of poppy fire,
Pavements as wide as play, unnerving roads,
Moon-scraping streets, advancing higher and higher
Against the hills. I can remember swords
Of crinkled lightning, followed by the dire
Threats of the thunder-slap, the loud-mouthed gods.

What wheels above the ironwork of pits
Stirred like a witches' cauldron in a spell
Of sweating muscles, wielded shovels, picks,
What tunnellers along the fringe of hell.
The stony lungs convulse, the wry mouth spits
As gravestones tell of tales they cannot tell!

The ocean with white froth upon its lips
Slobbers with ice-cream chops along the shore.
Afar, afar the creak of masts, the ships
Crowding white sails where sea-gulls wheel and soar
Above the bearded pirates. O the trips
Of sailors' bones across the jewelled floor!

Sandcastles in the sun and candy floss . . .
Gritty and sticky symbols of the child.
Steady the rolling stone, remove the moss
From thirty years. For once the world was wild,
Original, a chocolate-coated cross
A little boy bore on his back and smiled.

The Dead

D. Gwenallt Jones

With his fiftieth birthday behind him, a man sees with fair
    clarity
  The people and surroundings that made him what he is,
And the steel ropes that tether me strongest to these things
  In a village of the South, are the graves in two cemeteries.

I'd ride a bike pilfered from scrap, or with a pig's bladder
  Play rugby for Wales; and all that while,
Little thought I'd hear how two of my contemporaries
  Would spew into a bucket their lungs red and vile.

Our neighbours they were, a family from Merthyr Tydfil,
  The 'martyrs' we called them, by way of a pun,
And five of them by turns had a cough that crossed the
    fences
  To break up our chatter and darken all our fun.

We crept in the Bibled parlours, and peeped with awe
  At cinders of flesh in the coffin, and ashes of song,
And there we learnt, over lids screwed down before their
    time,
  Collects of red revolt and litanies of wrong.

Not the death that goes his natural rounds, like a gaol
    warder,
  Giving notice in the clink of his damp keys,
But the leopard of industry leaping sudden and sly
  That strikes from fire and water men to their knees.

The hootering death: the dusty, smokeful, drunken death,
  Death whose dreadful grey destiny was ours;
Explosion and flood changed us often into savages
  Fighting catastrophic and devilish powers.

Mute and brave women with a fistful of bloodmoney,
   With a bucketful of death, forever the rankling of loss,
Carrying coal, chopping wood for a fire, or setting the
      garden,
   And more and more reading the Passion of the Cross.

This Sunday of Flowers, as we place on their graves a bunch
   Of silicotic roses and lilies pale as gas,
Between the premature stones and the curb yet unripened,
   We gather the old blasphemings, curses of funerals past.

Our Utopia vanished from the top of Gellionnen,
   Our abstract humanity's classless, defrontiered reign,
And today nothing is left at the deep root of the mind
   Save family and neighbourhood, man's sacrifice and pain.

(trans: Anthony Conran)

The Public House

Rhys Davies

Opposite his home was the great public-house, a stone building edged with bright yellow bricks. The boy liked the public-house. It was clamorous with life, its interior brilliant with coloured bottles and vivid with a harsh smell; the movement of humanity in it interested him. After the staid cleanliness of his home it was satisfying to be allowed entrance, particularly in the early winter evenings, when the pink-speckled gas-lamps were lit and the floor was golden with fresh sawdust and crisp fires burned in the big grates.

He had right of entrance through friendship with the publican's sister, a gaunt spinster of forty who wore much coarse lace about her bodice, a black velvet band firmly binding a high mass of gold hair in which was a strange tint of mildew-green. Generous and lively, she spoke to him in a jokingly rancorous way as if he were a grown-up, and gave him pieces of mint-toffee and often a penny. But sometimes she lifted him and stood him on the bar counter, oblivious of the men in the saloon, and, clasping his bare knees with her big moist hands, she would ask him laughingly if he loved her and would he love her always, for ever and for ever. She could make him grin, and because her manner was raucous, he was not offended or humiliated. Yet she made him feel cautious too, and he experienced a vague, unformulated feeling when she gripped his knees and, lifting him down from the bar counter, her hands lingered about him. She was a strong woman.

"I don't think the boy ought to get into the habit of going into that public-house," he heard his mother say.

"God bless my soul," replied his father, "he's too young to know even what they're for."

"He'll get so used to a bar—" she went on.

"Well, perhaps he'll go into the business. There's money in pubs, Dorothy. And we'd have brandy and things cost price, if not for nothing."

An aloof friendship existed between the two families, though

21

the one was chapel-going and the other, being publicans in the strict nonconformist place, was cast out in pagan darkness. The ladies gossiped when they met on the pavement and at Christmas exchanged pieces of each other's puddings, one never failing to compliment the other on being more successful than herself. The boy's father, anxious to retain the pub's orders for decoration and painting, sometimes sat on one of its stools and slandered politicians with the publican, a bald widower who looked out on life from the grave of a ruined digestion, eating nothing but frail biscuits and watered-down soups.

"Your boy'll be a preacher," said the publican, surveying the child, who was kneeling behind the bar rearranging some rows of brown bottles.

"He doesn't look a preacher kneeling down among those stouts," chuckled the father. "What makes you think so?"

"His mighty looks at us, as if he's taking us all in and finding us wanting."

Vaguely the boy heard and half understood. He got up from his knees and stared absorbingly at the warm gold of a whisky-bottle. He liked to hold the smooth cold bottle and shake up the colour. There was the icelike gin too, and the purplish-red of the port, the tawny depths of the sherry; and strange seldom-touched bottles that were startlingly .green, white like curdled milk, yellow like buttercups, a red-black like beetroot, and a whitish-gold like sunlight. He stared at them all in turn, lingering for quite two minutes over each. So absorbed was he that he did not see the publican's sister approach and stand, hands on hips, gazing at him as absorbingly.

"Well, my lord, which'll you have?"

He started, pulled from his dream, and saw her large gaunt nose thrust out to him, the nostrils twitching with amusement. A sudden feeling of recoil gripped him, so that he was hard and unyielding when she swept him up into her arms, exclaiming:

"One day you shall have them all. On your wedding-day. You know what that is? Ah! Your wedding-day!"

The power of her physical warmth and dominant voice encircled him. He wriggled and was subjected. She tickled his ribs and he burst into wild laughter. He slipped to the floor and kicked out his legs. When his father, rapping his empty glass on

22

the bar counter, called out: "Now then, whiskers, time to go home," he jumped up with great alacrity and ran headlong past the rows of stout and out into the hall-way. There he joined his father, who was spitting into an enamelled pan marked *Spit Here.* Hand-in-hand they crossed the road and entered the grey evening silence of home.

He liked the public-house on Saturday evenings. Then it was bustling and overflowing with people relaxed from the tension of the finished week and determined to enjoy themselves. It reeked of a life that seemed to sprout with raw vigour like some great healthy cabbage. The windows steamed, all the gas-lamps were ablaze, even the big unappetizing "Commercial Room" was filled with a noisy mob of swollen-faced men. He wriggled his way among a forest of thighs, now and again darting right between a pair of men's legs, accompanied perhaps on these occasions by another boy: they played hide-and-seek among the crowded bodies. The publican's sister had no time for him on Saturday evenings. But sometimes she allowed him to climb on to a chair inside the bar and peer over into that narrow dark section of the pub reserved for women. It was shut-away and secretive, that section, and always shadowy, having no lights of its own. These drinking women fascinated him; they appeared only on Saturday nights; they squatted over their glasses of black stout and talked in low whining voices; they seemed to hide under large dark hats and they wiped their noses on the backs of their hands. There seemed something mournful about them.

Whenever there were apple-fritters Miss Sanders invited him to tea. He ate of them prodigiously, in the sitting-room behind the bar which, to his great surprise, was like anybody else's sitting-room, containing neither rows of coloured bottles nor sawdust on the floor. Sometimes, after tea, Miss Sanders would play the piano and sing in a deep voice *Oft in the Stilly Night.* She would then turn to him and say in a bantering way that she sounded like a cockerel. Her voice was a hoarse contralto. Once, when it was time for her to go to the bar, she asked him if he would like to screw on her ear-rings for her, but he was so awkward at the job that she did not repeat the invitation. She smelled of violets and the back of her neck was brown as an autumn leaf. But, in spite of the apple-fritters, he preferred being in the public-house proper to sitting there at the back with Miss Sanders.

One afternoon he was playing on the river bank with another boy. They quarrelled, the boy gave him a push and he fell into the water. His opponent, frightened, ran off. But he had only squelched into some mud, dirtying himself up to his waist. Indignant and alarmed, he gazed in horror at his slimy legs and knickerbockers. How was he to get himself dry and clean before going home! Some particularly unpleasant punishment would be given him if he went home like this. And quickly he thought of his friend Miss Sanders, who never criticised him and would only laugh at his state.

By roundabout back-lane ways, not daring to show himself in the main street, he reached the back of the public-house, scrambled up its wall and dropped into the yard. He crept down some steps and peered into the sitting-room window. Yes, she was on the sofa reading a book. He tapped nervously at the window; in his miserable wet state he dared not go to the door. When Miss Sanders had got him inside, her mouth gaped and she screwed up her eyes with laughter.

"Can you," he stammered, "can you give me a pan for me to wash my knees? And then I'll stand in front of the fire and get dry."

She stood in the middle of the room, her arms lifted, both her hands holding the high tower of her green-gold hair; she was looking at him meditatively now, having stopped laughing. "You come with me," she said at last. And she patted his head, took his hand and drew him upstairs. The swish of her hard shiny skirts was full of determination.

What a big bathroom they had! And it was white and splendid and not like the poked-away corner of the one in his home. Miss Sanders was turning on the taps in the enormous bath; he did not think anything; he gazed inscrutably before him. Briskly, with quick firm gestures, Miss Sanders took hold of him and whipped off his jersey.

He stood very still but once, as if trapped, he gazed round wildly at the door. Miss Sanders's well-known arms, hard and brisk with power, encircled him. They dexterously peeled off his clothes. He was clammy and shivering, and he was overcome with some strange new feeling that presently solidified into a knot of resentment in his mind. Too late! She had got him into the bath.

She rolled up her sleeves and, telling him that presently they would have some nice hot tea and pineapple together, she soaped him. There was no denying her. Busily, talking all the while with a bright hard gallop of words, she kneaded and rubbed his flesh. The resentment swelled into anger. At home he washed himself without help now. But he could not bring his tongue to protest. She had the large high power of the adult, and before this she had always behaved as a friend.

"There now, there now, all white and clean again! My word, look at the water! Eh, your mother would have carried on, I'm glad you came to me first . . . I'll wrap this hot towel round you, and you must wear a little jacket of mine till your clothes are dry . . ." She had lifted him out and was drying him vigorously, kneeling before him now, her breast oppressively against his face.

He did not enjoy his tea, sitting in the woman's jacket. Something had changed. He kept on gazing straight into the bunch of snapdragons on the table, eating with grave austerity and refusing a second helping of pineapple. He was glad when the publican came into the room. When his clothes were dry, Miss Sanders insisted on dressing him. Once she glanced sharply into his face and said:

"You mustn't be frightened, your mother won't be angry now. We won't tell her if you like."

And she pushed two pennies into his hand. He saw that she was in extraordinary good temper, her grey eyes, under which were mauve patches, bright-edged as diamonds. The bar was open as he made a slow almost funereal way through it. A resolve was at the back of his mind but did not declare itself: he made his exit with only a vaguely troubled emotion.

For he never returned to the public-house. Daily it was before him, bright and tempting and full of gaiety. He scudded past its steps, kicked a ball on its pavement, played marbles in the road before it. Garlanded with light in the evenings, the piano in the "Commercial Room" sometimes rollicking out its strident songs, men singing, tales told in the bar, snatches of mysterious phrases over which he used to ponder interestedly — he ignored and forsook them all. He regretted the loss. The public-house had been a whole world of marvels and attractive discoveries, and he remembered that part of it with pleasure. And then something happened which made it disagreeable, which ought not to have entered into that particular world. One afternoon as he strolled along the pavement, an upstairs window opened and Miss Sanders popped out her head.

"Hello, there, hello!" she called. "Why haven't you been to see me lately, you bad boy?"

Hesitating, he looked up but did not answer. She was smiling down at him, a smile of friendly mockery. He remembered thinking that the tower of her hair was in danger of toppling over. She was leaning out in such great eagerness, her bantering smile thrown down to him invitingly. He looked at her with curiosity but had nothing to say. Again asking for an explanation, she added:

"Well, at any rate, come in now. I want to talk to you."

He did not move. Suddenly she dropped a coin to him. "There's sixpence for you!" she cried, her smile breaking into a laugh. "Now come in to see me."

Picking up the sixpence, he began to slowly walk away, without comment, even to himself. He only remembered that for a long time he had wanted a certain penknife. Miss Sanders did not call out again, and when he reached the corner he made a sudden headlong dive out of sight.

The Mountain Over Aberdare

Alun Lewis

From this high quarried ledge I see
The place for which the Quakers once
Collected clothes, my fathers' home,
Our stubborn bankrupt village sprawled
In jaded dusk beneath its nameless hills;
The drab streets strung across the cwm,
Derelict workings, tips of slag
The gospellers and gamblers use
And children scrutting for the coal
That winter dole cannot purvey;
Allotments where the collier digs
While engines hack the coal within his brain;
Grey Hebron in a rigid cramp,
White cheap-jack cinema, the church
Stretched like a sow beside the stream;
And mourners in their Sunday best
Holding a tiny funeral, singing hymns
That drift insidious as the rain
Which rises from the steaming fields
And swathes about the skyline crags
Till all the upland gorse is drenched
And all the creaking mountain gates
Drip brittle tears of crystal peace;
And in a curtained parlour women hug
Huge grief, and anger against God.

But now the dusk, more charitable than Quakers,
Veils the cracked cottages with drifting may
And rubs the hard day off the slate.
The colliers squatting on the ashtip
Listen to one who holds them still with tales,
While that white frock that floats down the dark alley
Looks just like Christ; and in the lane

The clink of coins among the gamblers
Suggests the thirty pieces of silver.

I watch the clouded years
Rune the rough foreheads of these moody hills,
This wet evening, in a lost age.

Merthyr Vale and Aberfan — Valerie Ganz

Cadi Hughes

Glyn Jones

Upstairs in number one Colliers' Row, Ifan Cariad was dying by inches. People often say 'dying by inches' without really meaning it, but as a description of Ifan it was almost literally true; because his left leg was gangrenous to the knee and every day for the last week when Cadi his wife went upstairs to dress it and clean it out she found a new hole, sometimes the size of the palm of her hand, in a different part of his leg or the flesh of his foot. Then yesterday two of his toes had come off into her apron. The disease had started as a small piece of bad skin under the ball of the big toe, and it would soon pass upwards over the knee into his thigh; and then, when his whole leg had become putrid, it would separate from the rest of his body at the hip and lie discarded in the bed beside him. But Ifan would probably be dead before then, poor chap, unless a miracle happened.

Most of the time he was lying sog after the dope the doctor was giving him daily to ease the pain. His face in a short time had become yellow as clay and tiny, hardly bigger than a hand, with his nose rising up tight in the middle like a plucked fowl's breastbone. They had cut his hair short for comfort, and it looked like the pile on black velvet or plush, and fitted like a cap on top of his little monkey-face. And he had become so thin that his body lifted up the bedclothes hardly at all. He never was very much but he had shrunk to nothing. For days he hadn't eaten a bite, and all that had passed his lips was the water that Cadi fed him with out of the spout of the teapot. The smell of cooking nearly made his inside jump out of his belly, but one day near the end he whispered, "Cadi, give me something to eat."

"Of course, little Ifan," she said, humouring him, "what will you have?"

"I'd like some of that dinner I can smell cooking."

"Oh, you can't have that, little Ifan," she said, "that's the ham boiling for the funeral."

She was like that, always planning and scheming. She did everything possible for him; it suited her. She wouldn't let the district nurse come near, and when she wasn't actually fussing round him she would pray, or sing hymns in the voice she used when there were strangers in the chapel; not the nice modern hymns about Jesus and harps and rest beyond Jordan, but savage old-time stanzas by cracked Welsh poets preoccupied with punishment and corruption. She was wonderful the way she waited on him. But she had nearly killed him with her bossiness during the twenty years of their married life. When Ifan married her she was worth looking at; she wasn't just pretty like so many of the dark little women with heavy bottoms living in the mining villages, she was a beauty, big and straight, with blue eyes and hair the colour of a new penny. Ifan himself was small and dark; he looked wicked, a handful for any boss, the sort that always smells foul air in the pit and sees too much water in the workings quicker than anybody else, and makes trouble among the men generally. He was all there; and he knew the Mabinogion backwards.

As for her, she had no idea of her own beauty. All she wanted was for things to go on smoothly as she planned them. Anything odd, strange, eccentric, she hated like poison. And Ifan was a bit odd, what with his politics and his vegetarianism. He was a hot socialist but if he went on the stump she held herself off from him and gave him hell. And she didn't just stop with her tongue either. Poor Ifan wasn't much of an agitator in his own house; he had to draw his horns in at number one Colliers' Row or he could look out. She was a holy terror, bossing everybody and making arrangements all round, and turning out such a fuss-arse, and so trivial. And yet Ifan couldn't do without her; he was always a bit soft on her, imagining her, because of her hair, like Rhiannon or Blodeuwedd, or goodness knows who. And he could always think with pleasure of their courting days when the village boys going about in groups used to sing after the courting couples strolling up towards the lonelier roads:

> Red are the shivvies and red are the hips,
>> Hazel nuts are brown;
> Two of us climb up the Pandy tips
>> And three of us come down.
> Hoo!

There were more verses.

It was then he got his nickname. He was really Ifan Hughes, although everybody called him Ifan Cariad, which signifies Ifan the Lover, or Ifan the Sweetheart. He used to tap at the window of her house at night when he was calling for her, and her mother would call out from inside, "Who is there?"

"Ifan," he would answer.

"Which Ifan?"

"Ifan the lover of Cadi."

The neighbours heard, and such a chance for a nickname seemed like a godsend. He became known as Ifan Cariad Cadi, Ifan the lover of Cadi, or Ifan Cariad. But such a name in the village was never taken as a sign of disrespect. Everybody else had a nickname anyway.

Sunday morning, just as it was getting light, Cadi came into the bedroom to see if he was still alive. It was a bitter raw morning with no sun and thick clouds _crêped_ like slab rubber over the sky. He was all right, but just as she was going back to bed someone started knocking hard at the front door. Cadi was surprised, it was so early. She leaned over the banister and saw someone standing outside the figured glass panel she had had put in the middle of the door to best her sister-in-law. It was just a big dark shape, she couldn't tell who, although she stood there guessing instead of going to see. She slipped a petticoat over her head and got into a jacket of Ifan's, shouting, "Who's there?" There was no answer but the knocking started again, louder this time as though it wasn't going to stop in a hurry.

She opened the door.

It was God.

He was tall, dressed in a dirty green tweed suit with patch pockets and leather buttons but not much better than rags. There was a sack pinned round his shoulders, and on his head was a cloth slouch hat with the brim turned down over his eyes. His clothes were so disreputable, and yet he looked big and splendid somehow. His left leg finished at the knee, and he hugged a rough wooden crutch as thick as a bedpost, with some of the bark still on it, not padded at all, and spreading out like petals at the end. His grey beard was long but rather thin, and much of his skin was covered with red blind boils like rivet heads. His face was handsome though; patriarchal and majestic, but a bit seedy, and his hair was on his collar. She knew him all right.

"Let me in, Cadi," he said. He was her boss.

She did so, and upstairs he went sprightly enough, and straight into Ifan's room. There was chaff on his back and horse-dung on the heel of his boot.

"What do you want with us, little God?" she asked upstairs, rather anxious. He and Ifan were smiling at one another, knowingly, as though they had something good up their sleeve.

"I've come for Ifan," he said, still smiling and hardly looking at her.

Although she half expected it, it was a good bit of a shock to hear him say it straight out like that. "O little God," she began, sobbing, "don't take Ifan; I can't live with my brother, his wife quarrels with me, and I'm too respectable to be a washer-woman or go to the Big House."

Ifan grinned. He was a bit pinker than he had been, and more arrogant already.

"I must take him all the same," said God.

He stood his crutch against the commode and sat on the edge of the bed, quite at home, like a preacher. His eyes were cunning and very bright, with the skin drawn in all around as though his visit were a bit of a lark. He took very little notice of Cadi except to glance at her sometimes with his spotted eyes. She had more or less gone to pieces; all her bossiness and importance had got flat. She snivelled and started to whimper again.

"Take my daughter, Esther Cariad," she moaned, "she's unemployed and hard for us to keep."

"A cup of tea before we go, please," said God. "No fear," he continued, "it's not I'll be coming for her, Cadi."

Ifan nodded and looked serious.

She hung about whimpering for a bit and then went downstairs almost gladly to make the tea, and when she returned Ifan was sitting on the side of the bed dressing, with his huge bandaged leg hanging over the edge. She set the tray down hurriedly and started off on another tack. "Little Ifan," she pleaded, going up to him, "don't go and leave me, and me so good to you always."

Ifan looked at God, one leg in his trousers.

"Not so good, Cadi," he said, putting his saucer down.

"Indeed I have, little God," she answered reddening, "you don't know. I've nursed him hand and foot in illnesses and accidents, and pinched myself in the strikes for him and Esther."

"Ay I know," he said, "but what about having the bile on Labour Day, and throwing his Cheap Editions on the fire, and hiding the pennies for the gas so that he couldn't read at night, and keeping him home from his meetings to do the garden? You're a bitch, Cadi."

She smiled hoping to humour him. "It was only a bit of fun," she said; and seeing Ifan in difficulties over some vital buttons she was bound to go and help him.

"Very humorous," said God. "Anyway, come on, Ifan, get on my back. Cadi, thank you for the nice tea. We must be shifting."

She could see they were going in good earnest. She was red and serious again and desperate. "Don't go," she cried. "Ifan, stop. Let me get you a clean nightshirt first, then."

"Lay off," said God, "you'll tip us."

"Plenty of nightshirts where I'm going," said Ifan grinning. "Good-bye, Cadi."

Downstairs they went, not too badly. When they were in the passage, seeing them going for good and all, Cadi shouted down over the banister, "Ifan, have you got a clean handkerchief?"

God put him down quickly in the oak chair Cadi had in the passage for fashion and came headlong back upstairs. He swung at her with his crutch and hit her into the corner by the chest-of-drawers. She lay there in a heap without a sound, her mop of hair half down and her false teeth hanging out of her mouth.

God and Ifan hurried out of the house as fast as they could go, shutting the glass panelled door with a bang behind them.

from The Sound of the Wind that is Blowing

J. Kitchener Davies

You went down to Tonypandy for the Strike and the General
Strike,
for the jazz carnival, and the football of strikers and police,
to the soup-kitchens and the cobbling,
the jumble-sales for sore-ridden Lazarus,
helping to sweep the spare crumbs from the boards for the dogs
under the tables,
pouring alms like rubble on the tips
or sowing basic slag on allotment gardens of ashes
to cheat the arid earth into synthetic fertility.
    Then the hedges had fallen and the gaps were gaping
and the narrow streets were like funnels for the whirlwind's
pouring, blast upon blast,
to whip the corners and raise the house-tops,
whirling wretches like empty chip-bags
from wall to post, from gutter to gutter;
the cloudbursts and the hailstones choking every grating
splitting the pavements and flooding through the houses,
and clanging like a death-rattle in the windowless cellars;
and famine like a stiff brush sweeping through the homes
from front to back and over the steep garden-steps,
down the back-lane to the river's floods,—
the wrack and black water pouring from the cwm,
to be battered and spewed to the level land's hollow banks,
rubbish abandoned to rot.
    And there you were like Canute on the shore,
or like Atlas in a coal pit
with your shoulder under the rocks holding back a fall,
or with your arms outstretched between the crag and the sea
shouting "Hey! Hey!"
in the path of the lunatic Gadarene swine.

Remember,
there was no need for you, more than the rest of your fellows,
to scream your guts out on a soap-box
on the street-corners and the town squares;
no call for you to march in the ranks of the jobless,
your dragon-rampant hobnobbing with the hammer-and-sickle;
there was no need for you
to dare the packed Empire and the Hippodrome on Sunday
evening,
—you a dandy bantam on the dung-heap of the spurred cocks
of the Federation and the Exchange—
but you ventured,
and ventured in elections for the town Council and the County
and Parliament all in good time
against Goliath in a day that knows no miracle.
    Yes, I confess that I tried to hurl myself
into the whirlwind's teeth to be raised on its wings
and be blown by its thrust where it willed
as a hero to save my land.
Since it not only blows where it will, the tempest,
but blows what it will before it where it will;
"Who at its birth knows its growth," I said.

O shut your mouth with your lying self-pity
and your false unctuous boasting.
You know it was a giddy game with squirrels
to slip from bough to bough;
and a more reckless game to hover in the wind
like a paper kite, a string tying you safe to the ground,
where the crowd gathered to marvel at your feats
on the pantomime trapeze and your clowning in the circus.
Not riding the whirlwind, but hanging to the mane
of a little roundabout horse, that was your valour,
a child's wooden-horse in a nursery,
and the sound of the wind no more to you than the crackle of
        recorded music from vanity fair's screeching machine.

(trans. Joseph P. Clancy)

from Times Like These

Gwyn Jones

(The approaching General Strike of 1926 casts a long shadow over events in Times Like These. *Originally published in 1936, Gwyn Jones' novel is set in the Gwent mining village of Jenkinstown. Shelton is a wealthy official at the Cwm colliery and — together with his wife Louise, a local businessman called Broddam, and half the population of the Valley — he has come to Cardiff for an international rugby match. Of particular interest to the watchers from Jenkinstown is Ben Fisher, a miner at the Cwm today playing at outside-half for Wales. By now, tension between workers and management is approaching its height.)*

The crowd was by no means still. Where the gangways came up on the popular side there was a constant movement and change, and occasionally, to the accompaniment of screams and shouts they saw the remarkable and perilous swaying that character-ised Cardiff Arms Park at that time. There were not enough barriers, the crowd was not sufficiently divided, and as a result there were directions of pressure ending in between two hundred and a thousand spectators losing all control of their feet and weight. If you were in one, you suddenly felt a flooding of bodies at your back, tried to brace yourself, felt your feet leave the terracing, and away you went, sometimes completely off the ground, sometimes at a sort of running stumble, in a dreadful, helpless lurch. "Whoops!" the swayers cried, and "There she goes!" came from the excited onlookers. When at last the sway had spent itself upon broad backs or the railings in front, there was a lesser progress backwards, and then settlement again. "They should be able to stop that," said Broddam, and explained to Mrs. Shelton how such swayings occurred. "How dreadful!" she exclaimed. Above the heads of the mass floated a light blue fringe of tobacco smoke. Then they started singing, desultorily, keeping different times in different parts of the ground, to a tune different from that the band was playing. An old white-headed man waving a stout stick ran out from the ringside seats, and began to conduct with great sweeping

37

strokes. First one group, then another, joined in, made contact, surrendered themselves, and forty thousand voices in one mighty choir sent "Cwm Rhondda" pouring through the restless air. Some were singing in English, some in Welsh; chapel, church, and disbelievers — "Bread of Heaven, Bread of Heaven, Feed me till I want no more — Feed me till I want no more". They sang like men who find heartsease in singing, sustained and chant-like. More than two thirds there were from the hills and valleys, and in their voices one felt the austerity of toil, the passion of mountains under the stars, the sadness and grinding of their crude livelihood. The tune was changed. "Jesu, Lover of my Soul—" whitehead announced in a high, lilting voice, and the regimental band was with him. Louise, prepared to scoff, grew still and tense. Much that she had found in this people — its meanness, ugliness of life, and oftentimes savage hypocrisy — for the time she forgot, at the stupendous outpouring of this cry of sorrow for the New Jerusalem. The hymn died away like a universal supplication — and then came comedy. The next song dissipated religion and tears together. "Sospan Fach," cried whitehead, and only half the band could play for him. The gates had been shut long before this, and the kick-off was near. When they sang the Welsh national anthem, all those sitting in the stand rose, and most took off their hats. Louise rather resented this. It was like standing for the Marseillaise or something equally foreign. Yet, when the words had been twice sung, there were tears in her eyes. The ocean-swell of sound flooded the sky, poured into the thin blue, and was oddly over. Then it was time to start.

The Scots came on first, generously, even uproariously greeted, and then came the glorious scarlet of the home team. This was rapture.

"There must be a couple of hundred from the Cwm here to-day," Shelton told his wife.

Personalities were pointed out. Carbright—fastest man in the game; Fisher—standing by the gaunt forward — Bob Llewellyn — best forward playing to-day; MacAndrew and Burns, their halves; Seaforth and Tom Rees, the backs. The whistle blew. Gaels and Celts combined to sing the national anthem, and then the game started, Scotland playing from the river end. Without much success Louise tried to follow her husband's explanations. She heard that Scotland had scored after ten minutes and again after half an hour, but what she really enjoyed was the way the two packs set at each other towards the end of the first half. It needed no technical knowledge to appreciate this elemental matching of strong men. Patricians are never slow to turn down their thumbs. Skuse, that mighty blacksmith's helper, came staggering through in front of the stand, three men clinging around his neck and waist. She saw his chest heave up and out, and then he crashed like a tree, dragging his parasites with him. They all wriggled clear, and he scrambled up, his jersey in ribbons. Off it came, and there was the bulk of the man, his back light brown, with red blotches from the scrummages, his barndoor chest clotted with black hair. As his arms went up into the sleeves of his new jersey, there was a rolling of muscles throughout his torso, a rippling of elastic and steel. Bulges came out across his round ribs, a pattern of power and drive. "Shouldn't care to stop him!" Shelton grunted. "By gad, no!" echoed a stranger next to him. For the present Skuse was Shelton and the stranger; they were Skuse. So the hammering went on. Minutes wore themselves to tatters, and play had finally settled in the Scottish twenty-five. A long, muttering roar played over the banks and stands. There was a scrum down under the posts, MacAndrew put the ball in, it came out slowly on the Scottish side, held in the back row, Llewellyn broke away from the scrum, threw himself at MacAndrew as he gathered the ball, it bounced back awkwardly, Shand snapped it up and drop-kicked as he was sent sprawling. The ball hit an upright, there was a groan, bounced on to the crossbar in a deathly silence, and fell over for four points amidst a howl of triumph.

"Eight-four," Shelton explained. "Shand dropped a goal — that's four points." He saw with delight that his wife was adding her handclap to the applause.

There was no further score before half-time.

The second half was desperately hard. Laughter, groans, chatter, cheers, objurgations, some drinking from bottles brought into the ground, and several horrible swayings, showed that the crowd was on its toes. "Come on, Wales!" Louise heard a clear tenor voice shouting from behind the Scottish line: "You'm playing towards the pubs, ain't u?" There were stoppages. "Man out!" Rees had crash-tackled Magraw. A little man in a cloth cap ran on with a sponge, the water dripping as he ran, but before he reached the place of combat Magraw was up, shaking his big head. "Gertcher!" jeered the crowd, and the little man ran back again, with his hand held high. The forwards played murderously — one moment bearing down with the inhuman pressure of a steam-roller, the next, disintegrated, crashing and sprawling. Louise found herself looking for Ben, and cried sharply as he came through the centre, slick as a slice of fat bacon, was forced sideways, and finally hurled winded into touch. They rubbed his belly, shoved his head between his knees, he shook himself like a dog, and the game went on. Six minutes to go. The game settled on the Scottish line. A good touchfinder carried play back to the twenty-five. Three minutes to go. Shand took a long line out. The players seemed to have straggled halfway across the field. Llewellyn jumped up as though he would tear down Olympus, grabbed the ball, and flung it back. Wretchedly it was kicked ahead to Burns, who sliced his kick away to the right. For a moment no one seemed interested in the ball, all the players seemed to be standing still, and then the ground was pandemonium. A figure in a scarlet jersey was coming from nowhere at the ball. It was Fisher. "By Great God Almighty," someone yelled behind Louise, "he's going to get it!" Seaforth, too, ran for the ball, and the most knowing held their breath as they saw that he was going to fly kick. As his boot drove forward, Ben dived for the ball, insanely, got his hands to it, missing death or injury by an inch. His body was flung across Seaforth's knees, and the full back went down with a screech. But Ben was up, running with his head back, like the madman he was. He saw Burns in front of him, checked himself, stumbled almost on one knee, cleared him in a queer, doubled-over fashion, pulled himself upright, and then, as Magraw caught him by the thighs and Johnson by the head, threw the ball hard and true inside him to Shand, who took the ball on his chest and was over the line for a try under four forwards. Three men were out at once — Fisher, Shand, and Seaforth with a twisted knee — but it was a try. You could hear the row all over the town. Strangers hit strangers' hats off. Men punched each other for joy. No one was sitting down; there had been an unparalleled lurch towards the one corner, and dozens of spectators were overcome by the pressure. It was almost an anticlimax when Tom Rees and Llewellyn arranged the ball as carefully as if it were a big diamond, and Tom, deaf to the crowd, inhumanly cool, took his short run and deftly kicked the two points that brought the score to nine-eight and a victory for Wales.

"We've won!" cried Shelton, on his feet like the rest.

"I'm so glad!" said Louise, who had forgotten with her husband that they were English.

As they waited to leave the stand, Shelton heard Sir Hugh's advice again. "You go to the Park and cheer your head off, if you want to, and then go back to the Cwm like a sensible fellow and see if you can't knock sixpence off Fisher's payroll."

from The Deluge, 1939

Saunders Lewis

From Merthyr to Dowlais the tramway climbs,
A slug's slime-trail over the slag heaps.
What's nowadays a desert of cinemas,
Rain over disused tips, this once was Wales.
Pawnshops have closed their doors. Clerks
Of the labour exchange are the chiefs of this prairie.
All flesh has tainted its way on the face of the earth.

The same taint's in me, as I second proposals
In committee after committee, to bring the old land to life.
I'd maybe be better employed on a Tonypandy corner
And my eyes meditating up the valley and down
On the human wreckage adrift in the mire of despond,
One function common to man and the standing slag.

Eyes have been changed to dust, we know not our death,
Were buried by our mothers, had Lethe milk to drink.
We cannot bleed, no, not as former men bled,
Our hands would resemble a hand, if they'd thumbs to go on
                                                  them.
If a fall shatters our feet, all we do is grovel to a clinic,
Touch our caps to a wooden leg, Mond pension and
                                                  insurance:
Knowing neither language nor dialect, feeling no insult,
We gave our masterpiece to history in our country's M.P.s.

(trans. Anthony Conran)

from We Live

Lewis Jones

(Lewis Jones was a Rhondda miner, an active trade unionist and a member of the Communist Party. Published in 1939, his novel is based on his experience of strikes, lock-outs and political meetings in the South Wales coalfield. In this extract, the main character, Len, has just been arrested during a demonstration against the local Labour Council's inability to provide adequate parish relief and school meals during the General Strike of 1926.)

Hours later Len was lifted roughly from the stony floor of the cell into which he had been flung. He vaguely sensed he was being dragged along a dark passage, but didn't take much notice. He wondered if he had two heads and how far apart they were from each other. He knew they were on fire because of the fierce burning in them. His eyes pricked him like red-hot needles and he was afraid to open them, but the bright light in the room to which he was taken seeped through the lids and forced them open. The momentary glance showed him, through a steamy mist, a large number of uniformed men. He raised a heavy hand to his head, then dropped it again, wet and sticky, to his side. A murmur of dim voices came to his ears, but he made no effort to distinguish what was said as his knees began to wobble and he crumpled face down upon the floor.

The next thing he remembered was the sound of low moans and a trembling that shook his limbs like jelly. He slowly gathered his thoughts and drew himself to his knees, all the time wondering what had happened and where he was as he rose unsteadily erect. His head still throbbed, but the burning agony had gone, although his ears were filled with a funny buzz that somehow made him think of the mountain in summer. He stood swaying for some seconds, then thrust his arms before him and stepped out — one pace, two paces — before his knees touched an obstruction. Bending down, he let his fingers run over the coarse cloth that covered something like a bench. Straining his eyes to see what was there, he fancied the air became lighter, and looking at the floor behind him he saw a shadowy pattern beginning to form on it. He kept watching this, his whole soul in his eyes, until he distinguished black bars with panes of light between them.

Slowly lifting his head, he saw the small window high up on one side of the cell wall. Turning away, he gazed around the cold emptiness that surrounded him before wearily making for the bench to sit down. The clammy air made him shiver, but he did not think of the blanket beneath his body as, with his head clasped in his hands, he drew to his mind all that had happened. His eyes filled with tears as he again saw Mary in the grasp of the huge policeman and the bodies of his mates upon the wet earth.

A thin, squeaky noise, percolating from the street into the cell, disturbed the painful soliloquy. Len listened and heard a newsboy shout "Special Edition." The sound made him happier in a moment, as it gave him contact with the world outside. He thought it sweeter than the music of his mountain larks and walked hurriedly to the cell window the better to catch every syllable.

"Russians imprison British subjects." He stretched himself taut at the words and breathlessly waited for the rest. "No free speech in Russia. Englishmen in danger. The Government takes stern measures."

Len wondered what had happened and for a moment forgot his own predicament. He slowly resumed his seat upon the plank, and as he thought more deeply over the newsboy's cry a bitter smile curled his lips.

He never remembered how long he sat without moving, but he suddenly felt the cold steal through the flesh into his bones. He shivered and pulled the solitary blanket over his shoulders in an effort to keep the cold at bay. Finding this insufficient and his muscles beginning to quiver involuntarily, he rose and paced the cell, the blanket dangling to his feet like a robe. The rhythm of the walk began to work itself into his brain, which made a song of each step. "Eight steps up. Stop. Five steps across. Stop. Eight steps up. Stop." He sat down again to get away from the maddening reiteration, and tried to retrace the events of the day. But tales he had heard of what policemen did to prisoners in the cells insisted upon intruding into his thoughts. The affair of Syd Jones the wrestler came to his mind with stunning force. He remembered the night Syd was frog-marched to the station and brought out next morning dead from heart failure. Big Jim always insisted the man had been beaten to death. Other incidents and anecdotes crowded into his mind, where they became a panorama of living pictures that bred in him a slow-developing fear. He looked about the cell for a weapon, but saw nothing, and suddenly realised it had become pitch dark. He sat down again, closing his eyes tightly in a vain attempt to shut out the pictures that passed before them.

He began wondering what the police intended doing with him. His imagination illuminated the cell and he saw the iron-studded door open to admit a number of great hazy forms. He jumped up in a frenzy, only to find the darkness more intense than ever. Fearing to sit down again, he paced the cell once more. This time the thud-thud of his tramping feet made him think of boots and he smiled when he remembered the old saying that all policemen had big feet. But the smile faded into a pitiful twist of the lips with the thought that boots made fine weapons. Better than batons, he thought, when a man was down. He saw them, big, black, and shiny, staring at him from all parts of the cell, and their cold, glittering hardness appalled him. He felt them driving into his head and body, and closed his eyes to sweep them from sight. But they followed him, scores of them, lifting, falling, kicking, thudding. "No-no," he shouted hysterically, burying his face in his arms. "Not that, not that. You can't kill me here."

His breath came in gasping sobs and he sat down to steady himself. The thick darkness seemed to press on him, but when he raised his head he fancied the walls had drawn closer together. Perspiration ran in trickling streams down his face and the hair on the back of his neck bristled. He stopped breathing and tried to brace himself, but all the time the walls came nearer and nearer, until he felt they were nearly on him and ready to crush him in a clammy embrace.

He sprang erect in a panic and raced to the door, which he missed in the darkness, flattening himself against the opposite wall. Rebounding from this, with increasing panic he hurled himself in the opposite direction, and sensing he was against wood began to kick madly at the door, at the same time screaming: "Let me out! Let me out! For God's sake let me out! I'm smothering."

There was no answer and he kept on kicking and screaming until, when he was nearly exhausted, he heard the shuffle of feet outside the door and the clanging of keys. He felt the door pressed open against his body and retreated more deeply into the cell, where a flash of light suddenly blazed full on his eyes, completely blinding him.

"What the bloody hell is all this fuss about?" he heard a voice ask roughly.

The sound and the knowledge there was another human being with him sent Len's courage back to him in surges. Still seeing nothing, he pulled himself erect and answered: "Nothing. I only wanted some company."

For a second there was amazed silence, then:

"You cheeky little bastard!" came the indignant retort.

from Gwalia Deserta

Idris Davies

O what can you give me?
Say the sad bells of Rhymney.

Is there hope for the future?
Cry the brown bells of Merthyr.

Who made the mineowner?
Say the black bells of Rhondda.

And who robbed the miner?
Cry the grim bells of Blaina.

They will plunder willy-nilly,
Say the bells of Caerphilly.

They have fangs, they have teeth
Shout the loud bells of Neath.

To the south, things are sullen,
Say the pink bells of Brecon.

Even God is uneasy,
Say the moist bells of Swansea.

Put the vandals in court!
Cry the bells of Newport.

All would be well if—if—if—
Say the green bells of Cardiff.

Why so worried, sisters, why?
Sing the silver bells of Wye.

from Gwalia Deserta

Idris Davies

The village of Fochriw grunts among the higher hills;
The dwellings of miners and pigeons and pigs
Cluster around the little grey war memorial.
The sun brings glitter to the long street roofs
And the crawling promontories of slag,
The sun makes the pitwheels to shine,
And praise be to the sun, the great unselfish sun,
The sun that shone on Plato's shoulders,
That dazzles with light the Taj Mahal.
The same sun shone on the first mineowner,
On the vigorous builder of this brown village,
And praise be to the impartial sun.
He had no hand in the bruising of valleys,
He had no line in the vigorous builder's plans,
He had no voice in the fixing of wages,
He was the blameless one.
And he smiles on the village this morning,
He smiles on the far-off grave of the vigorous builder,
On the ivied mansion of the first mineowner,
On the pigeon lofts and the Labour Exchange,
And he smiles as only the innocent can.

Little Fury

Gwyn Thomas

We were in Standard Three. Mr. Peachey was our teacher. He was small; he had his thin yellow hair plastered as consciously as trellis work over his head to lessen the effect of baldness. He made a long journey each morning to school from some point well to the south of the valley. Into the classroom at the beginning of the first lesson he brought a huge package of food and a thermos flask. As the first lesson advanced he would vanish once a minute behind the blackboard for a gulp and a swallow. He was not a genteel eater. We would stare at the blackboard, fascinated, while the racket of his chewing went on. We were often hungry ourselves and would have wished to join him in this noisy carnival of appetite.

He was a good disciplinarian. If at any time during his retreat behind the blackboard a boy took a liberty and made a noise his head would shoot into view, his jaws working mightily and his eyes swollen and watery from the strain of trying to dispose of his latest mouthful.

The first lesson of each day was Religious Instruction. Mr. Peachey was no theologian. He seemed most of the time to be proceeding on the scraps of Scripture he himself had picked up as a boy, and he was not helped by the fact that this was the lesson in which he did most of his serious eating. His method was to call the roll of the best-known characters in the Old Testament and ask us who they were. The simplest reply from us would suffice, and it brought a grunt of approval from Mr. Peachey, locked in struggle with his sandwiches behind the blackboard.

"Who was Moses?" . . . "Leader."
"Who was Elijah?" . . . "Good man."
"Who was Jezebel?" . . . "Bad woman"
"Who was Naboth?" . . . "Wine-grower"
"What happened to Naboth?" . . . "Stoned."
"Who saved Isaac?" . . . "God and a goat."
"From whom did the goat save Isaac?" . . . "Jacob."

"Who demolished Jericho?" . . . "Joshua."

"With what instruments?" . . "Trumpets."

From that point on the morning would go forward in a kind of coma of toleration. We, bored or vigilant, Mr. Peachey digesting.

Then the reign of pleasure ended. It was a Wednesday morning. The early morning assembly had gone all wrong. We had been given a new hymn and we had not struck a single right note on the first few runs through. It was a favourite hymn of the headmaster, Mr. Tobias, a stout man with a desperately red and angry face. He had stopped in the middle of the second verse of our last attempt and dismissed us in three words: "Disgusting! Turn! March!"

And out of the hall we marched, sullen, ashamed.

We got to the classroom. Mr. Peachey registered us and retreated to his position behind the blackboard, already champing like a stallion. It was one of the quickest starts we had ever seen him make. In the third minute of the lesson Mr. Tobias appeared, leaning into the room, his fingers white with strain on the door-knob, his face the image of an outraged bull.

"Mr. Peachey," he began, and stalked right into the room. Mr. Peachey cringed, kept flattening his hair on his head and his jaws maintained their invariable chewing. We all leaned forward in our desks, the wood hard and assuring against the pity and terror in our hearts.

"There is a place for eating, Mr. Peachey," bawled Mr. Tobias. He had his mouth open and his arm upraised for a whole series of shattering commandments. Then Mr. Peachey gave a sharp little cry and hurtled out of the room. I thought I could hear the sound of relief that came from our tensed minds.

Mr. Tobias looked around the room. He was eager to expend all his anger there and then. He was not easy in his own mind. There seemed a hint of embarrassment and contrition in the glances he cast at the door through which Mr. Peachey had just vanished.

He concentrated his attack on the desk in which I sat. It was a desk made for three. I sat at one end, Lloyd Treharne at the other and in the centre our friend Willie Nuttall. I could feel Willie's body against mine, rigid with anxiety. His hands were over the desk in front of him, clenched and dirty. Willie was our special friend. We knew that outside the school, as we played among the ferns on the hilltops or stretched out to talk on the hot metal plates of the stoke-hole of the steam fan at the bottom of our street, Willie was nowhere near as dense or slow as he became once he put his foot inside the school. He was the eternal victim, the everlasting butt.

Mr. Tobias flung his finger out at us. He rattled off three problems in simple mental arithmetic. Lloyd did his. I did mine. It was on a theme of purchased herring that had become as familiar to us as sun and moon. But from Willie Nuttall came a shiver of torment, then a silence as total as that of death. Mr. Tobias raved and stood with one hand over Willie's head, but when Willie turned his face up to him, the pale skin utterly whitened by his dumb anguish, Mr. Tobias' hand did not descend and again his eyes shot at the door through which Mr. Peachey had passed, as if his little gesture of mercy with Willie eased his feeling of having in some way erred in the matter of Mr. Peachey.

Then Mr. Tobias examined us swiftly in Scripture. We did as well as we could. Lloyd and I kept our hands on Willie's shoulder, encouraging him to be wise and bold like the older people we saw on the earth. This time he broke silence. Mr. Tobias' jaw dropped as he heard some of Willie's answers. Jericho had gone to heaven in a golden chariot. Genesis had been stoned to death in his own vineyard. Jezebel had been turned to salt.

"And who betrayed Samson?" asked Mr. Tobias.

"The Lilac," said Willie, inspired by the feel of our hands on his shoulder to speak out more loudly than usual.

Mr. Tobias laughed a gale. He was delighted to have done with his wrath and cruelty and he overdid the laughter. The sound of it and the sight of his purple, straining face we found stranger than his rage. Willie's defeat and inertia were now complete. He sat between us as still as a boulder, his eyes of glass. Lloyd and I sensed a change in him. He had become sinister, in his tiny way, threatening.

"He fell off a wall, sir," said Lloyd, blurting his words out.
"Who, Samson?"
"No, sir. Willie, sir. Willie Nuttall. He fell off a wall."
This was the story that Willie had told us to explain the

strange seals of silence that would suddenly slip into place inside his head.

Mr. Tobias threw up his arms comically. He was still eager to have us fill our ears with the tiny bells of clowning he had stitched on to the dark cloak of his knowing and mastery. Then suddenly the bells were torn off, he hardened back into exile and left the room.

Within a minute Mr. Peachey crept back, looking more haunted and bitter than ever. He stood by the window and stared at the perfect quality of light on the steep hillside that stretched to the west. He was wishing himself there, totally illumined and at peace. His jaws kept working in their endless athletic hunger. We heard a sound from beyond the door which was half plain glass. Miss Ilfra Desmond, the teacher from the class next door, stood there. She looked in at Mr. Peachey with a pity and affection that almost melted the glass. She had been looking at Mr. Peachey with that same expression ever since she had come to the school two years before, but he had remained in his grey little cell of aloofness. Miss Desmond was a woman of about thirty-five, Mr. Peachey's age. Even we sensed the great warmth of her heart and the tormented loneliness of her days. She had come to our valley from Somerset early in life, had learned Welsh perfectly in order to express her emotional kinship with the people who speak it and was now its most zealous teacher in the whole school.

She moved her feet on the granite slabs of the corridor outside the door to attract Mr. Peachey's attention, but he was deaf with his misery and did not heed her. She passed down the corridor and he continued to stare at the mountainside. "Now," he said very quietly, "we shall have the poems."

These were the poems he made us learn by heart, a different one for each boy. These poems were the only peak of delight in Mr. Peachey's life.

"Lloyd Treharne," he said.

Lloyd began Mark Antony's oration, and he stood squarely in the aisle to give himself plenty of room for gestures. With this recitation, especially the look of magnificent sorrow that transfixed his face when he flung out his finger at the coffin of the dead Caesar, he was an almost permanent winner of the threepenny prize at the Penny Readings.

When he finished Mr. Peachey remained silent for some seconds, playing with the window cord and muttering to himself: "The good is oft interred with their bones, their bones, their bones . . ." He jerked his head up as he felt the probing of our wonder into his mood. "Willie Nuttall," he said

Willie stood up.

> "It was a summer evening
>   Old Jasper's work was done
> And he, and he, and he . . ."

That was as far as Willie ever got. He had found the poem inscrutable from the start.

"Sit down, Nuttall," said Mr. Peachey. "We all know what happened to Jasper anyway. One day some fool is bound to bring you a skull too and ask you what about it. Nathaniel Ellis."

That was myself. Mr. Peachey never failed to call on me for the sad short poem he had made me learn. It seemed to be his favourite. I spoke it out in a voice I hoped would be as rich and commanding as Lloyd's Mark Anthony:

> "Rose Aylmer, whom these wakeful eyes
>   May weep but never see,
> A night of memories and of sighs
>   I consecrate to thee."

There were tears in Mr. Peachey's eyes as he listened, and he rubbed the window cord into his brow as if to blunt and assuage some lacerating thought that had camped there for ever.

The bell rang. Mr. Peachey left our room and Miss Desmond came in for the special Welsh lesson. We were the children of Welsh-speaking parents from whose tongues the language had for some reason vanished. The echoes of the ancient speech stirred in the far back of our minds but our lips knew it not. Miss Desmond approached us with a mixture of sympathy and an apostolic urge to repair a great wrong. She had found what we had lost and she was anxious to restore it to us.

She cast a glance at Mr. Peachey as they passed at the door but he stared straight ahead, still lost in his trance of failure and discontent.

Miss Desmond's voice was sharp as she began the lesson, a

strange thing for her, for she was fond of us. She concentrated her fire on Willie Nuttall. He had that effect on people. He sat in the room's dead centre, crouching down and seeking only to be left alone. But if malice were abroad it took the hint at once and started on Willie.

Miss Desmond tried to put him through the primal and static simplicities of the grammar's first pages. *Y mae'r bachgen yn yr afon.* The boy is in the river. *Y mae'r cath-ar y bwrdd.* The cat is on the table. *Y mae'r fuwch yn y cae.* The cow is in the field. Stark stuff, but just right for us.

Not a word came from Willie. Miss Desmond leaned over him. There was a faint odour of lilac about her. Grief had pressed her face that morning into a small tremulous shadow. She beat on Willie's flattish nose with a long yellow pencil. Lloyd and I sat edgily, waiting for the first deadly rumble.

Then it came. Willie gave a loud witless roar. Lloyd and I jumped from our seats to let Willie into the aisle. He leaped on to the desk and in three jumps reached the front of the class by way of the other desks, creating a chaos of terror and ink. He ran into the corner where the T square stood. He started brandishing it like a club. He advanced on Miss Desmond. His face was expressionless and like chalk. Miss Desmond felt the draught of the down-swinging T square. She fled from the room with a shriek, Willie after her. Lloyd and I and two or three more followed. We saw Miss Desmond haring across the yard. Willie was about six feet behind her, lunging demonically. Then from a side-door, looking unusually spruce for him, dressed in P.T. kit, came Mr. Peachey. He burst into the hardest sprint I ever saw. Miss Desmond fell helplessly against a brick wall. Willie braced himself for the final act of rebellion and wrath, then was hurled flat on his face on the yard's concrete surface as Mr. Peachey caught his legs in a flying tackle.

Mr. Peachey lifted Willie to his feet. Willie was crying.

"Not there. Not there," he shouted, pointing at the school. He broke from Mr. Peachey's grasp and slipped through a gate that led out on to the hillside. We went after him, just Lloyd and I, for we were his good friends.

We sat with Willie for a while in a little hollow on the hillside. It was our own secret refuge, a place of cool tranquility. Then we made our way down to the steam fan at the bottom of our street, where the old engineer, Mr. Davey, put us to sit in the stoke-hole on the hot metal plate and watch him as he fed the furnaces. Mr. Davey had a bag of apples and a round of tales from the sea which he shared with us. Our fear flaked away and we laughed and in no time we were talking delightedly of our constant dream, the cottage on the mountain's crown and the numberless dovecots we would build for our eternal sanctuary when we made our final escape from the perplexities of the valley bed.

At dinner time we jumped startled to our feet. Into the stoke-hole came Mr. Peachey himself. He gave us sixpence each. "It's all right," he said. "It'll be all right." He was smiling.

Nothing was said to us when we returned to school. When the last class ended we followed Miss Desmond and Mr. Peachey down the hill home. They walked slowly and he was bending over her with an arrogance of assertive wanting that rebuked the timidities which seamed our hills. We hastened our step and we winked and nodded at them in a conspiracy of encouragement. "It'll be all right," he called to us.

And on the few occasions after that when I recited —

> "Rose Aylmer, whom these wakeful eyes
> May weep but never see . . ."

I saw not a trace of sadness on his face, nor yet on the face of Miss Ilfra Desmond, for whom a new life would appear to have begun from that day.

The Ballad of Billy Rose

Leslie Norris

Outside Bristol Rovers' Football Ground —
The date has gone from me, but not the day,
Nor how the dissenting flags in stiff array
Struck bravely out against the sky's grey round —

Near the Car Park then, past Austin and Ford,
Lagonda, Bentley, and a colourful patch
Of country coaches come in for the match,
Was where I walked, having travelled the road

From Fishponds to watch Portsmouth in the Cup.
The Third Round, I believe. And I was filled
With the old excitement which had thrilled
Me so completely when, while growing up,

I went on Saturdays to match or fight.
Not only me; for thousands of us there
Strode forward eagerly, each man aware
Of tingling memory, anticipating delight.

We all marched forward, all, except one man.
I saw him because he was paradoxically still,
A stone against the flood, face upright against us all,
Head bare, hoarse voice aloft, blind as a stone.

I knew him at once, despite his pathetic clothes;
Something in his stance, or his sturdy frame
Perhaps. I could even remember his name
Before I saw it on his blind-man's tray. Billy Rose.

And twenty forgetful years fell away at the sight.
Bare-kneed, dismayed, memory fled to the hub
Of Saturday violence, with friends to the Labour Club,
Watching the boxing on a sawdust summer night.

The boys' enclosure close to the shabby ring
Was where we stood, clenched in a resin world,
Spoke in cool voices, lounged, were artificially bored
During minor bouts. We paid threepence to go in.

Billy Rose fought there. He was top of the bill.
So brisk a fighter, so gallant, so precise!
Trim as a tree he stood for the ceremonies,
Then turned to meet George Morgan of Tirphil.

He had no chance. Courage was not enough,
Nor tight defence. Donald Davies was sick
And we threatened his cowardice with an embarrassed kick.
Ripped across both his eyes was Rose, but we were tough

And clapped him as they wrapped his blindness up
In busy towels, applauded the wave
He gave his executioners, cheered the brave
Blind man as he cleared with a jaunty hop

The top rope. I had forgotten that day
As if it were dead for ever, yet now I saw
The flowers of punched blood on the ring floor,
As bright as his name. I do not know

How long I stood with ghosts of the wild fists
And the cries of shaken boys long dead around me,
For struck to act at last, in terror and pity
I threw some frantic money, three treacherous pence —

And I cry at the memory — into his tray, and ran,
Entering the waves of the stadium like a drowning man.
Poor Billy Rose. God, he could fight,
Before my three sharp coins knocked out his sight.

from The Citadel

A. J. Cronin

(THE CITADEL follows the career of Andrew Manson, who arrives as a newly-qualified doctor to practise in a mining community in south Wales in the 1920's. He soon finds that his working conditions are impossible and the health of his patients at constant risk from outbreaks of typhoid due to an inadequate sewerage system. Encouraged by his wife Christine to gain better qualifications, he goes to London to take his exams.

In the following extract, he has just returned to Wales elated with his success, when he is informed of a pit disaster.)

When the train got in, half an hour late, it was nearly midnight. All the way up the valley the engine had been battling against a high wind and at Aberalaw, as Andrew stepped out on the platform, the force of the hurricane almost bowled him off his feet. The station was deserted. The young poplars planted in line at its entrance bent like bows, whistling and shivering at every blast. Overhead the stars were polished to a high glitter.

Andrew started along Station Road, his body braced, his mind exhilarated by the batter of the wind. Full of his success, his contact with the great, the sophisticated medical world, his ears ringing with Sir Robert Abbey's words, he could not reach Christine fast enough to tell her joyously everything, everything which had taken place. His telegram would have given her the good news; but now he wished to pour out in detail the full exciting story.

As he swung, head down, into Talgarth Street he was conscious, suddenly, of a man running. The man came behind him, labouring heavily, the noisy clatter of his boots upon the pavement so lost in the gale he seemed a phantom figure. Instinctively Andrew stopped. As the man drew near he recognised him, Frank Davis, an ambulance man of Anthracite Sinking No 3, who had been one of his first-aid class the previous spring. At the same moment Davis saw him.

"I was comin' for you, doctor. Comin' for you to your

house. This wind's knocked the wire all to smash." A gust tore the rest of the words away.

"What's wrong?" shouted Andrew.

"There's been a fall down at Number Three." Davis cupped his hands close to Manson's ear. "A lad got buried there, almost. They don't seem to be able to shift him. Sam Bevan, he's on your list. Better look sharp, doctor, and get to him."

Andrew took a few steps down the road with Davis, then a sudden reflection brought him up short.

"I've got to have my bag," he bawled to Davis. "You go up to my house and fetch it for me. I'll go on to Number Three." He added, "And, Frank! — tell my missus where I've gone."

He was at No 3 Sinking in four minutes, blown there, across the railway siding and along Roath Lane, by the following wind. In the rescue room he found the under-manager and three men waiting on him. At the sight of him the under-manager's worried expression lifted slightly.

"Glad to see you, doctor. We're all to bits with the storm. And we've had a nasty fall on top of it. Nobody killed, thank God, but one of the lads pinned by his arm. We can't shift him an inch. And the roof's rotten."

They went to the winding shaft, two of the men carrying a stretcher with splints strapped to it and the third a wooden box of first-aid material. As they entered the cage another figure came bundling across the yard. It was Davis, panting, with the bag.

"You've been quick, Frank," Manson said as Davis squatted beside him in the cage.

Davis simply nodded; he could not speak. There was a clang, an instant's suspense, and the cage dropped and rocketed to the bottom. They all got out, moving in single file, the under-manager first, then Andrew, Davis — still clutching the bag — then the three men.

Andrew had been underground before, he was used to the high vaulted caverns of the Drineffy mines, great dark resounding caves, deep down in the earth where the mineral had been gouged and blasted from its bed. But this sinking, No 3, was an old one with a long and tortuous haulage way leading to the workings. The haulage was less a passage than a low-roofed burrow, dripping and clammy, through which they crawled, often on their hands and knees, for nearly half a mile. Suddenly the light borne by the under-manager stopped just ahead of Andrew who then knew that they were there.

Slowly, he crept forward. Three men, cramped together on their bellies in a dead end, were doing their best to revive another man who lay in a huddled attitude, his body slewed sideways, one shoulder pointing backwards, lost seemingly in the mass of fallen rock around him. Tools lay scattered behind the men, two overturned bait cans, stripped off jackets.

"Well then, lads?" asked the under-manager in a low voice.

"We can't shift him, nohow." The man who spoke turned a sweat grimed face. "We tried everything."

"Don't try," said the under-manager with a quick look at the roof. "Here's the doctor. Get back a bit, lads, and give us room. Get back a tidy bit if I were you."

The three men pulled themselves back from the dead end and Andrew, when they had squeezed their way past him, went forward. As he did so, in one brief moment, there flashed through his head a memory of his recent examination, its advanced bio-chemistry, high sounding terminology, scientific phrases. It had not covered such a contingency as this.

Sam Bevan was quite conscious. But his features were haggard beneath their powdering of dust. Weakly, he tried to smile at Manson.

"Looks like you're goin' to 'ave some amb'lance practice on me proper!" Bevan had been a member of that same first-aid class and had often been requisitioned for bandage practice.

Andrew reached forward. By the light of the under-manager's lamp, thrust across his shoulder, he ran his hands over the injured man. The whole of Bevan's body was free except his left forearm which lay beneath the fall, so pressed and mangled under the enormous weight of rock, it held him immovably a prisoner.

Andrew saw instantly that the only way to free Bevan was to amputate the forearm. And Bevan, straining his pain tormented eyes, read that decision the moment it was made.

"Go on, then, doctor," he muttered. "Only get me out of here quick."

"Don't worry, Sam," Andrew said. "I'm going to send you to sleep now. When you wake up you'll be in bed."

Stretched flat in a puddle of muck under the two foot roof he slipped off his coat, folded it, and slipped it under Bevan's head. He rolled up his sleeves and asked for his bag. The under-manager handed forward the bag and as he did so he whispered in Andrew's ear:

"For God's sake hurry, doctor. We'll have this roof down on us before we know where we are."

Andrew opened the bag. Immediately he smelt the reek of chloroform. Almost before he thrust his hand into the dark interior and felt the jagged edge of broken glass he knew what had occurred. Frank Davis, in his haste to reach the mine, had dropped the bag. The chloroform bottle was broken, its contents irretrievably spilled. A shiver passed over Andrew. He had no time to send up to the surface. And he had no anaesthetic.

For perhaps thirty seconds he remained paralysed. Then automatically he felt for his hypodermic, charged it, gave Bevan a maximum of morphine. He could not linger for the full effect. Tipping his bag sideways so that the instruments were ready to his hand he again bent over Bevan. He said, as he tightened the tourniquet:

"Shut your eyes, Sam!"

The light was dim and the shadows moved with flickering confusion. At the first incision Bevan groaned between his shut teeth. He groaned again. Then, mercifully, when the knife grated upon the bone, he fainted.

A cold perspiration broke on Andrew's brow as he clipped the artery forceps on spurting, mangled flesh. He could not see what he was doing. He felt suffocated here, in this rat-hole, deep down beneath the surface of the ground, lying in the mud. No anaesthesia, no theatre, no row of nurses to run to do his bidding. He wasn't a surgeon. He was muddling hopelessly. He would never get through. The roof would crash upon them all. Behind him the hurried breathing of the under-manager. A slow drip of water falling cold upon his neck. His fingers, working feverishly, stained and warm. The grating of the saw. The voice of Sir Robert Abbey, a long way off: "The opportunity for scientific practice . . ." Oh God! would he never get through!

At last. He almost sobbed with relief. He slipped a pad of

gauze on the bloodied stump. Stumbling to his knees he said:
"Take him out."

Fifty yards back, in a clearing in the haulage way, with space
to stand up and four lamps round him he finished the job. Here
it was easier. He tidied up, ligatured, drenched the wound with
antiseptic. A tube now. Then a couple of holding sutures.
Bevan remained unconscious. But his pulse though thin was
steady. Andrew drew his hand across his forehead. Finished.

"Go steady with the stretcher. Wrap these blankets round
him. We'll want hot bottles whenever we get out."

The slow procession, bent double in the low places, began to
sway up the shadows of the haulage. They had not gone sixty
paces when a low rumbling subsidence echoed in the darkness
down behind them. It was like the last low rumble of a train
entering a tunnel. The under-manager did not turn round. He
merely said to Andrew with a quiet grimness:

"That's it. The rest of the roof."

The Doctor

John Tripp

His old bullnosed Morris with the canvas roof
chugged onto the pavement, badly parked.
We heard his wheeze a full minute up the path
before he appeared, bulbous-purple-veined
in a shiny suit, flopped trilby, stained tie
and the permanent Player stuck to his lip.
Grey ash dropped off to the greased lapel
and waistcoat, as he opened his worn bag
containing pills, a flask and stethoscope.

Sometimes his Scotch breath was a wall
buffeting us, unkind in its revolting fumes.
Often he was conscious of this formidable waft
and sucked an acid-drop from a flat tin.
His fingers would grip the rubbery tubes
of the scope, fix the earpiece, and the plate
slipped about on a racked chest or lolling belly.
He pawed too much, fumbling his rare gift
out of a whisky muddle, holding some dread

of sickness within him after the deadly years
in attending to it, of seeing them die.
He had asthma, well forward, whistling sadly
down pipes, snatching at the dry, primitive
inhaler, sometimes fighting for sweet gulps
of simple breath to keep him running.
He delivered the infants, and watched the miners
go, stretched out in tidy front rooms.
Nobody complained. We were too fond of him.

On mornings of fog, sleet, and torrential wet
we saw him erect inside his rattling cab
held together with hope, elastic, wire and string
as it shook along the terrace by day and night.
He was the Doctor, serving six forgotten

poor square miles, carrying his leather bag
wherever it was needed by his people,
sitting tight within the dignity of an oath
between the bad hours of his own sickness.

Disused Chapel — George Chapman

Smells

Islwyn Williams

I

The smell of Sunday. Not the snuffling-savoury richness of the meat browning in the Gough Road ovens as we walk home from the morning service, but the austere, the religious smell that makes me sneeze as I explore the darkness of the wardrobe-with-a-mirror in the front bedroom: camphor, with the faint whiff of lavender, sometimes near, sometimes far away.

To-night the lavender has gone, for my mother has left us in the darkness outside the chapel and I am sitting with my father in the vestry next door. They don't walk on tip-toe in here, and to avoid their grinning stares I press my face between the back of the seat and my father's side. It is the smell of the wardrobe. . . .

I withdraw cautiously from the sanctuary of his arm and look round. It is a low rectangular room with dingy, discoloured walls lit by four gas brackets, one of them hissing fiercely and making exactly the same sound as my grandfather does when he spits into the fire. On one wall there is a shiny picture of a man in a long nightshirt looking sadly at five lions; on the other a faded photograph of a one-eyed man looking very surprised and benign. It is very hot and stuffy, and for a few moments I watch drops of water trickling fitfully down the ribbed window-panes above my head. The room seems to be packed, with men crowding the seats on one side and women on the other, all talking furiously and laughing. At the far end, all by himself near the stove there is a dark little man with flashing eyes, looking very worried and impatient.

"Who are those fat women over there?"

"Those? Those are what they call the altos, *bach*."

"Who are these men?"

"Tenors they call us. I'm one of the tenors."

"What is —?"

The dark little man imperiously strikes the stove with his stick and speaks. The talk dies down, there is coughing and throat-clearing and the pages of the yellow books whisper. An oppressive silence. A piano begins to tinkle, slowly at first, then quicker and louder until — MY GOODNESS! I catch my breath violently as the room vibrates with loud voices. My father. My father is doing it! That isn't my father singing? Don't say that that is my father *singing!* Strong, high-pitched, nothing like his usual speaking voice; it is simply a loud penetrating yell. His body is shaking too, and his mouth — oh *mam fach!* — his mouth is wide open like a baby screaming. All right! That's silly; silly that is, and I shall tell my mother . . . the neck of the man in front of us is red, very red. A blue vein is moving, swelling, subsiding, swelling . . .

A sudden silence and everybody is talking again. My father smiles down at me and asks pleasantly if I had heard the singing. Heard it? *Heard* it? There is too much noise to say anything except "Yes." A man with a drooping white moustache but yellow near the lips turns round to ask me if I sang bass. Then he laughs hoarsely, almost soundlessly, except that it sounds like hundreds of little wheels whirring furiously in his throat. I ignore him completely and turn to my father.

"There's a thin woman over there now."

"Where?"

"She's with the fat women."

"But why, *bach*?"

"She's thin."

My father looks mystified, and then laughs loudly. He turns quickly to the man sitting next to him. . . .

II

They are always the same; every time I push open the glass door and smell the freshness of the soap and the not unpleasant acridity of burning hair, they come back to me. It was here I caught my first glimpse of the strange world beyond the village; a colourful and un-Welsh world, of teeming streets and high buildings; of screaming trams and the unending clatter of hooves; of men in light suits smoking scented tobacco and little yellow sailors padding silently by; of great multitudes crowding the pavements; of garish lights everywhere as we hurried for the train.

None of my mother's commandments. was easier to obey

than the one she would pronounce of a Saturday morning when she gave me fourpence to go and have a haircut. In the first place, it gave me a pleasurable feeling of superiority over my contemporaries, the poor chaps who had to submit to the indignity of their mother's apron and their father's ruthless clippers outside the back-door. (Years passed before I discovered that my distinction was simply due to my father's unbelievable lack of skill in using any kind of implement.) In the second place, it was a heaven-sent opportunity to linger awhile in the company of grown-ups talking freely on subjects of which I heard nothing whatsoever at home. The talk in our house was largely confined to family gossip (my mother was one of nine married sisters), sermons, and political speeches (there were photographs of Lloyd George and Campbell-Bannerman in the front room), and of course, eisteddfods and concerts and singing-school — all of them, as far as I could see, painfully boring. And even when something interesting did come up at the frequent family gatherings, my requests for further enlightenment were promptly crushed by the simple expedient of saying in an off-hand way that I didn't know them, that they came "from down the bottom there somewhere," and why didn't I go out to play for a little while? Yes, "down there somewhere" they always lived. Dear me, to think of the load of unmentionable sins that I have attributed to poor old Brick Row in my time.

It was an event, therefore, to go to the barber's shop, to be welcomed in the most friendly way by the barber in his long white coat, with his hair miraculously curled back like a gleaming black cornucopia above his forehead. There, too, I would find men who carried elegant walking-sticks, who wore straw hats and brown boots, and whose moustaches were immaculately pointed instead of drooping miserably like the bushy and undisciplined monstrosities of the deacons in our Big Seat. And if you happened to sit next to one of them on the black leather bench you might have a chance to have a good look at his fancy waistcoat. You leaned forward negligently and then glanced back carelessly over your shoulder; then you would be able to examine the wonderful buttons. They were usually made of glass and inside there were beautifully-coloured miniatures of foxes and greyhounds and birds and racehorses.

Oddly enough, my father would dismiss these people with a disgusted little jerk of the head and refer to them, for some peculiar reason, as "men of the world". Well, whoever they were, they were jolly interesting people. Talk! They talked of everything; of things like boxing and football, of holidays at Llanwrtyd and Llanstephan and Blackpool and London, and of the extraordinary things that went on in the Swansea Empire every week. It was from them that I first heard of Jim Driscoll and Freddy Welsh and Jack Johnson; of Percy Bush and Gwyn Nicholls and Willie Trew and Dicky Owen and Jack Bancroft; of Harry Tate and Marie Lloyd and Gertie Gitana; of the Crystal Palace and the Tower and the Giant Dipper and the Big Wheel. And the strange thing was that my parents knew nothing of all this; not only couldn't they discuss them intelligently, but they had never even heard of them!

How well I remember that never-to-be forgotten morning when there was general agreement in the room that the Jimmy Wilde who had won the great fight a few nights previously was the one and the same Jimmy Wilde who used to come to our village with the fair every year, and who, in fact, as the barber himself pointed out, had often sat *in the very chair* I happened to be occupying that morning! The thrill I experienced that moment was incomparably greater than that which I felt when I was lauded to the skies for reciting the 104th psalm at my first Sunday school anniversary. It appeared that someone had christened the new champion "The Ghost with a Hammer in his Hand," and as I walked home I meditated on what was generally agreed to be a brilliant description. Its meaning, however, had completely eluded me, and so I decided to ask my grandfather about it when I got home. In contrast to my parents, who were completely mystified by everything, my grandfather did know one or two things, and he would always have a good shot at explaining some of the meaningless jargon I used to hear from time to time in the barber's shop. If he didn't succeed in elucidating something on the Saturday he was usually able to clear up the matter on Sunday morning, much to my mother's disgust. But on this particular occasion, I remember, he was completely baffled, and after spitting thoughtfully into the fire several times, gave it up as something he would have to inquire into later in the day; for the moment he placed the phrase in the same category as those which had worried us on previous occasions, things like "Ten to one bar one", "Six to four in Jimmy o' Goblins", "Any to come", and similar mumbo-jumbo. . . .

Another exciting session was that at which I first heard of the great Chung Ling Soo. The barber himself used to visit the Swansea Empire every Thursday night, and on this particular morning, as was his wont, he was giving a very detailed account of what he had seen. A woman being sawn in two; a kettle from which Chung Ling Soo had poured anything in the way of drink that the audience had asked for; he had swallowed hundreds of needles only to extract them a few minutes later threaded on a length of cotton; he had shot a human cannon-ball up to the roof of the theatre. And then, to close the performance, he had walked to the front of the stage and had asked the conductor of the orchestra to open his mouth. . . .

"And by damn," concluded the barber, turning to me at last, "he jumped down his throat! *That* was how he left the stage!"

But when I arrived home with the story searing my lips, I was furiously annoyed to find my mother an uncompromising sceptic on the subject; she laughed most unpleasantly and received my account of the performance in exactly the same way as my father had received the information of mine a few days before that the Ystalyfera Rovers were expected to play Aston Villa on the Ynysydarren ground on Easter Monday: the same unhealthy and obstinate scepticism exactly. After dinner I brooded pityingly on how little, after all, my parents knew of the wonderful world around them, and how painfully out of touch they were with the things that really mattered. And I became increasingly bitter later in the afternoon as I came to realize how many hours, how many precious hours, my father had literally wasted in those confounded bookshops in Swansea when only a stone's throw away the doors of the Empire and the land of magic were open wide.

III

The excitement did not come all at once; it came gradually, almost imperceptibly. One morning I would wake and know it was there simply by looking through the window; there was a new sunshine, a new, a holiday disposition of blue sky and white cloud. And presently there would arise from the floor of the valley a strangely exciting fragrance, the mysterious incense that from that moment onwards would follow us everywhere: to school, to the Band of Hope, to chapel. It was a delicious mixture of smoke from steam-coal (strange to us who were used to anthracite), paraffin, and thick engine oil. Going on errands became a pleasure, for there were strangers in the village street: men with greasy clothes and grimy faces; in the shops were gaily-dressed women with dark complexions and thick black hair and long ear-rings (I never understood the scorn in my mother's voice when she spoke of someone being "dressed up like a showman's daughter"). In the still, morning air one could hear the noise of unloading and erecting, an occasional sharp shout, the thudding of wooden mallets. There was an air of festivity about that was infectious; the village suddenly acquired an air of urban sophistication, and as the Thursday afternoon half holiday approached the pulse of our lives perceptibly quickened. School became a torture, the common task doubly arduous.

The three-day fair had arrived.

After an eternity of waiting, Thursday would come at last, and with it, life being what it is, its own troubles. By then I had found it expedient to obey all my mother's orders with the utmost alacrity and dispatch. By then, too, I had found occasion to call on all my uncles and aunts within striking distance, and had weighed them in the balance. I remember the chagrin I felt once when, after running around most strenuously for an aunt of mine for a whole evening, she rewarded me with a packet of home-made sweets and a cap full of apples — a noble reward in ordinary circumstances, but how fantastically inappropriate, I thought, that particular week. I felt that it was not so much due to meanness as to a deplorable lack of imagination.

After dinner, during which I had been wondering whether half-past-two was a little too early and three o'clock was cutting it a bit fine, I would look expectantly at my mother.

The ritual would begin with my mother taking down her purse from the mantelpiece with a deep sigh. Sorrowfully she

71

would explore its hidden depths, and at last she would hand me a coin with the air of a martyr bowing to the inevitable.

Then it was my turn. I would take the coin on the palm of my hand, staring at it incredulously. Then, staggering back a step or two and catching my breath realistically, I would ask weakly:—

"Wh—what is this?"

My mother would reply in a matter-of-fact voice that it was money to go to the fair. It was far too much, of course, but still — what was I waiting for? Wasn't I going to the fair or what?

I would flop into a chair, completely overcome. She—she didn't mean that? She really didn't mean it?

Good heavens, of course she did. Where did I think the money was coming from? Did I think she was made of money or what? Or did I think she picked it up on the highway?

The scandalized astonishment that my mother could work into her voice as she asked these questions was only equalled by the mounting indignation in mine:—

What did she think I was? That was my reward, was it, for running around like a slave for weeks? What about the blackberries I had gathered the previous evening? Who had cleaned out the coal-house from top to bottom? And did she think I had joined the Bible class because I liked it?

The outcome usually was a compromise; my mother would hand me another sixpence, but on one condition: that I was to bring a shilling back. And if we had meat for dinner on Sunday, we'd be jolly lucky.

In any case, I had to be pretty cautious on the fairground. To buy chips or a piece of pink and white French nougat near the entrance on the way in was asking for trouble. And not for me, either, the desperate venture of trying to win a prize at houp-la or to knock down a cokernut; the pleasure was too short-lived and the reward too uncertain. I usually kept away from stalls of that kind.

But there was one exception. It was a shooting gallery. The girl stood in the same place every year, leaning negligently against the side of the stall with a rifle across her forearm. Her eyes were dark and brooding and her skin a golden brown. She had very thick and shiny black hair wonderfully coiled about her jewelled ears, and her teeth flashed whitely when she spoke.

72

At every fair I used to sidle up cautiously, just to feast my eyes on her. Once I crept too closely and she leaned forward eagerly to offer me a rifle at seven shots for a shilling. It was impossible, of course, and I skulked away with my ears burning, the most contemptible creature in the whole world.

On the whole, therefore, I believed in having a swing or a ride for my money. Besides, it was important to have enough money left to see the sideshows at the far end of the field, and above all, to be able to patronize the most exciting attractions of all. These were the travelling cinemas belonging to Messrs. Creecraft and Wadbrook, the wonderful electric bioscope. The main attraction, naturally, was the film show inside, but personally I was more than grateful for the free show on the outside stage before each performance. This took the form of a display of acrobatic dancing by the most beautiful women I had ever seen in my life. (Women, I repeat, in spite of the indelicate assertions of the Brick Row toughs in Standard Seven who used to go round saying that the dancers were actually men dressed up as women and that one or two of them had bald heads and smoked pipes and had hairy calves—faugh!) How well I remember the pleasure they gave me as they danced and pirouetted to the music of the magnificent organ behind them! I can still see them, bathed in the brilliance of the arc-lamps, I can still hear the light thud of their feet on the boards as they danced to the music of the organ with its hundreds of gilt and silver pipes, its toy figures in green and blue and peach, and especially the little fellow with the baton in the middle keeping perfect time with the clash of the cymbals and the unseen drums. I once remember one of my Sunday school teachers groping pitifully for words to describe the glory of the temple of Solomon when I knew all the time that he had only to say that it was like the front of Wadbrook's show.

On the last Saturday night the fair would be invaded by such crowds that my mother usually deemed it wise to accompany us. Not that my father was enthusiastic; far from it. His attitude to the fair was an unfathomable mystery to me; he openly confessed that he was bored by the whole thing, and could only be induced to come on the Saturday night merely to act as a sort of bodyguard. But I will say this for him: he was always prepared to conclude the visit by patronizing the electric bioscope, or "the living pictures," as he called them.

There were two ways to go into the show. First, there was the front way: you waited until the dancing was over, and then, as soon as the organ began to play 'God Save the King,' you scrambled up the steps, crossed the stage under the full glare of the arc-lamps, and rushed for the pay-box. Usually, however, a queue would be formed on the stage, and you would have to wait your turn; not an unpleasant situation, for from there you were able to greet your less fortunate acquaintances in the crowd below. And of course, this was the way that most people used. But then, as my father explained, they didn't know Mr. Wadbrook: he did. Apparently, Mr. Wadbrook thought the world of my father; it appeared that, quite unknown to me, they had been exceedingly friendly for years. And as a special privilege, only granted to close personal friends, my father was allowed to use the other entrance, the side door. The great advantage of using this side entrance, according to my father, was that, first of all, you avoided the wearisome task of climbing the steps; in the second place, you escaped the danger of being trampled to death in the rush for the pay-box; and above all, you avoided the cruel glare of the arc-lamps. Consequently, we always used the side entrance. Mind you, it was not so pleasant underfoot, and it was much darker, of course; in fact it was so dark that I personally considered it a danger to life and limb. But then, as my father was never tired of pointing out, compared to the risk of offending his old friend Mr. Wadbrook by refusing to take advantage of the privilege offered, the slight inconvenience of having to grope maddeningly in the darkness and the mud for the side entrance was nothing; it was a mere trifle. The great thing to be avoided was the harmful effect of the glaring lights, and to make perfectly certain of keeping on the right side of Mr. Wadbrook. Curiously enough, my father was a great personal friend of Mr. Creecraft as well, for he also allowed him to use the side entrance to his show.

Which only went to prove, as my grandfather used to remark sagely, that there *were* certain advantages in being a deacon — you got to know, among other things, charming and influential people like Mr. Wadbrook and Mr. Creecraft.

* * *

And so the fair would come and go away again. Early on Monday morning from my bedroom window I would look down at the fairground. By then the colourful tents and booths had disappeared and wisps of mist from the river would be trailing lazily among the skeletons of the shows. Drab pantechnicons and vans trailed slowly through the churned mud towards the exit and along the riverside road. The fair was going, and by the afternoon the ground would be empty and desolate, with nothing left except muddy patches of sawdust, the crazy rainbows of the paraffin puddles, and ragged papers eddying fitfully in the far corners. And as I gazed, I knew that for another six months the riverside would once again take on its air of rustic remoteness.

And that night as I looked down from my bedroom window, all would be dark and quiet down by the river; the fair as I knew it late at night would have gone: the orange night-sky above softly glowing with the suffused reflection of the myriad pinpoints of lights down below; the clangour of bells and missiles striking steel plates at the back of the stalls; the screams and the laughter; the strains of many competing organs, a confused but happy dissonance made wailful by the distance, now subdued, now strongly borne aloft to my home on the hillside by a capricious wind.

Mynydd Gilfach

Sam Adams

Along the mountain's haunch
The sheep track sidles, morsed
With droppings, black and round
As olives. The boy inside

Stepped nimbly in the battered rut,
And winter breath sang stinging
Down my throat, my duffle coat
No poet's cloak to stream

Romantically behind. Old Huw
Walked here, imperious and gaunt,
Oblivious of the miners he passed by,
Remote in his utopian dreams.

And Bob the Runner trained his lurcher
Bounding up these steep ascents;
No fancied greyhound ever raised
A finer spray of morning dew.

Today the tangled brambles
Are random heaps of rusty wire,
Scabrous traps for freezing air
And tufts of wool, Gorgon manes.

Outcrops of sheep are still
And grey as stones. The boy beside
Is running to the low spilled wall,
Rolling its lichen-gilded lumps,

Watching them come to rest
As grey and still as sheep.
The farmer's wire is here,
So taut it cuts the wind

In tunes. The two boys feel
The hurt within, and turn
To see projected on the mist
The shadow of their mountain.

The cwm fills up with evening,
Clotting round the terraces,
Lapping at the crenellated
Ranks of chimneys, row by row,
The loop of road, the central void.

from The Best of Friends

Emyr Humphreys

*(Published in 1978, this novel opens in Aberystwyth in 1928, where
Amy and Enid are first year students. Emyr Humphreys charts their
progress at university, showing how both girls become politically aware
and how their lives are altered by the men with whom they form
relationships. When Amy's boyfriend leaves Aberystwyth to work in a
Quaker settlement in the Valleys, Amy decides to follow him there.)*

The train was very late. It sniffed and shuffled its way deeper
into the valley. The steam hissed in the drizzle. The winding
gear at the pithead came into view. It stuck out of the mist as
threatening as a giant gibbet. Amy gazed apprehensively
through the window. Black slag heaps dominated the funereal
procession of terrace dwellings called to a permanent halt in the
narrow valley. The mountains above them were hidden in
cloud. In the far corner of the compartment a woman with a
thyroid condition protected a seven-year-old boy who lay
stretched on the seat, his school cap on his head which lay in her
lap. He was sleeping with his mouth open and her arm lay
across his chest. She had difficulty in keeping her arm still. Her
hand with the thick wedding ring on her sensitive finger
twitched with the desire to feel her son's hot forehead and move
the limp lock of hair. She studied the view on her side of the
carriage as intently as Amy studied the view on hers. Talking
would disturb the boy. Distaste for the view through the dirty
window mingled with concern for a son who could be ill.

The train jerked forward again. The engine seemed confused
by a sequence of contradictory signals. The mother clutched the
boy too tightly. He stirred and opened his eyes. Without
moving his head he catechised his mother in a parched babyish
voice.

"Are we there, then? Are we there yet, Mam?"

She bent her head to whisper to him soothingly, keeping a
calculating eye on the world outside. A row of ruined miners'
cottages came into sight. They had been abandoned when the

coal waste reached the back doors. She seemed to consider drawing the boy's attention to the sight and then to think better of it: even the ominous cocoon of mild fever was preferable to the grim reality outside the window. Above the ruined cottages a row of unemployed men and boys were on their knees turning over the slag and picking coal to put into sacks. The woman shifted in her seat. She found the sight of the ragged men on the side of the tip too embarrassing to watch. She looked at Amy as though to register her reaction. The boy was awake. She could break the silence in the compartment. A little talk might soften the stark surroundings. She seemed ready to snatch at anything that would bring a little warmth and comfort.

"People don't know", she said. "People don't realise. Not until they come here. The sheer misery. They don't understand."

The boy began to complain again. His throat was burning. He pressed his hand against it and seemed to consider crying. The mother bent over him, whispering urgently, begging him to be patient. They were almost in sight of the station. Once again the train ground to a halt. The woman looked at the drizzle outside and began to whisper explosively.

"I never wanted to come here," she said. "Never. I told my husband. It's not fair to the boy, I said, and it's not fair to you. One minister for two circuits. And most of the members unemployed. It's ridiculous, I said. Absolutely ridiculous."

Amy nodded understandingly. There was nothing else she could do. The journey had to come to an end: but they were still bound together like two strangers trapped in a tunnel sharing the same pocket of air.

"The day we arrived it was terrible. The sun was shining and you think that would have helped but there was coal dust all over the street. And the girl had left the front door open and the dust had blown inside. It was all over everything. And to crown it all a dog from the street had wandered upstairs and left his paw marks all over the white bed. I can tell you. I just sat down and cried."

Amy was doing her best to look sympathetic. The boy had begun to mumble disgruntledly. He wanted all his mother's attention. He made her bend down to catch his murmuring complaint. She smiled apologetically at Amy and brought her face as close as she could to his. When the train suddenly jolted forward their noses touched. The boy broke out into delighted laughter. Her expression was instantly transformed.

"You're better, aren't you?" she said. "My little boy is feeling better."

He jumped to his feet, tottering about drunkenly as the train moved forward in fits and starts. They were coming into the station. He shouted out the name on the signal box.

"Cwm Du Signal Box!"

And he caught the first glimpse of his father waiting for them in the shelter of the waiting-room door. He was a conspicuously neat figure in clerical grey and a trilby hat. He walked briskly alongside the moving train, his white hands raised ready to open the compartment door.

"Now then, Dad! Catch me! Catch me!"

Amy moved aside to allow the boy to jump out into his father's arms. While he still held his son the minister enquired in muted tones about his condition. Amy hurried down the platform to the luggage van at the end of the train. The guard was scratching his head as he looked at two large bales of old clothing.

"I don't know how you're going to manage," he said. "They're heavy, you know. They're heavier than you think."

The only luggage truck available was parked under the station canopy. Two children were sitting on it. It was a pleasant place to sit while they watched the train. One of the boys sat with his back to the track and studied it over his shoulder. When Amy bent down to pick up the long handle she saw that the boy's feet were bare. His companion wiped his nose on his sleeve and grinned at Amy encouragingly. When the truck was gone they scampered across the entrance to take up perches on the seat outside the waiting-room.

"Isn't there anybody here to meet you?" the guard said.

"They must have given up."

Amy looked determined to be cheerful.

"The train was so late."

The guard raised his eyebrows loftily, ignoring any implied criticism. With Amy's help he struggled to deposit the two bales on the truck. With both hands she dragged the load under the wooden canopy. The drizzle had stopped for the moment but the clouds were low. The rain could fall again at any time. The minister and his wife watched her with mild interest. He plucked out his watch from his waistcoat pocket and studied it carefully.

"Would you believe a train could be almost three quarters of an hour late? It's symptomatic, you see. We don't count. A decaying community. Left to one side and forgotten."

Barn Owl

Leslie Norris

Ernie Morgan found him, a small
Fur mitten inexplicably upright,
And hissing like a treble kettle
Beneath the tree he'd fallen from.
His bright eye frightened Ernie,
Who popped a rusty bucket over him
And ran for us. We kept him
In a backyard shed, perched
On the rung of a broken deck-chair,
Its canvas faded to his down's biscuit.
Men from the pits, their own childhood
Spent waste in the crippling earth,
Held him gently, brought him mice
From the wealth of our riddled tenements,
Saw that we understood his tenderness,
His tiny body under its puffed quilt,
Then left us alone. We called him Snowy.

He was never clumsy. He flew
From the first like a skilled moth,
Sifting the air with feathers,
Floating it softly to the place he wanted.
At dusk he'd stir, preen, stand
At the window-ledge, fly. It was
A catching of the heart to see him go.
Six months we kept him, saw him
Grow beautiful in a way each thought
His own knowledge. One afternoon, home
With pretended illness, I watched him
Leave. It was daylight. He lifted slowly
Over the Hughes's roof, his cream face calm,
And never came back. I saw this;
And tell it for the first time,
Having wanted to keep his mystery.

82

And would not say it now, but that
This morning, walking in Slindon woods
Before the sun, I found a barn owl
Dead in the rusty bracken.
He was not clumsy in his death,
His wings folded decently to him,
His plumes, unruffled orange,
Bore flawlessly their delicate patterning.
With a stick I turned him, not
Wishing to touch his feathery stiffness.
There was neither blood nor wound on him,
But for the savaged foot a scavenger
Had ripped. I saw the sinews.
I could have skewered them out
Like a common fowl's. Moving away
I was oppressed by him, thinking
Confusedly that down the generations
Of air this death was Snowy's
Emblematic messenger, that I should know
The meaning of it, the dead barn owl.

Tairgwaith

Bryan Martin Davies

Between the Steer tip and the Maerdy tip,
two of the sullen guards of my 'cynefin',
was Tairgwaith,
three streets of close houses,
grown, somehow, from the slag;
a piece of black Rhondda, swaggering boldly
on the green of Comin y Waun.

There was a park there,
some swings, a shoot and roundabouts,
ragged blonde-haired boys who spoke English,
and huge mothers wearing their husbands' caps.
They shouted loudly in protest
against children and still tips.
They smoked Woodbines from packets of five,
they also swore, sometimes.
We knew in some strange way
that they never went to Carmel or to Hermon either
on white Sundays.

We ventured there, like knights, on our broken bikes,
into the angry city,
knowing in our hot fear
that there were people here
who boiled Brynaman boys in brown boilers
on the kitchen fire,
and ate them eagerly for breakfast,
flinging their wet bones on to the gleaming slag;
but there we went,
into the land of these morose strangers,
because we were, after all,
Brynaman boys.

Tonight the paint of this landscape drips
over the frame.

(trans. Bryan Martin Davies)

In the Dark

Robert Morgan

"I wonder what's keeping that haulier," said Dan Thomas, "he should have been here thirty minutes ago."

He was sitting in a narrow dark road just high and wide enough for a horse and tram to pass to and fro. Over his broad, muscular shoulders hung his jacket like a cape and around his neck was draped his shirt like a scarf. The road was cold and damp with large knotted fungus, like fists, clinging to the road posts. Opposite the man sat a boy of fifteen, small and thin, who was curled up asleep. They had just finished a snack and were waiting for the haulier to change the full tram that stood at the coal face. Their lamps hung on posts above their heads, shining dull lights on the ribbed rock and rail track.

The haulier was late and the man appeared worried at the delay. He looked towards the sleeping boy curled up and almost invisible under a ledge of rock.

"Glyn," he called out to the boy, "Glyn, wake up, it's not good to sleep down here".

The boy did not move; his aching body had given way to a deep sleep. He lay oblivious to the man's words.

"Glyn," he called out again, getting up and touching the boy, "you'll get a chill; it's dangerous to sleep in the cold air."

He stared at the sleeping boy, bending over him and shining his lamp in the boy's face. He gently shook the boy's shoulder then straightened himself, took off his jacket and scarf, rolled them together and wedged them between two ledges of rock. The boy stirred, uncurled himself, and half opened his eyes.

"Come on Glyn lad, shake away the sleep, there's a lot to do."

When he saw the boy moving he hitched his lamp on his belt and walked to the coal face.

Glyn staggered to his feet. He wished he could sleep, to be left alone so that he could sleep . . . sleep. The thought of three more hours of work before going home shattered his thoughts. He slowly took off his jacket and shirt and threw them carelessly to the side of the road. He looked up at his lamp on the post and yawned long and despairingly; then he took his lamp from the post and walked slowly towards the coal face. He entered the coal face on his hands and knees and glanced at the seam of coal wedged hard between roof and floor. Dan was already working the seam, driving a mandrel-blade into the coal and prizing it to the floor. Glyn, half awake, and aching, took a mandrel into his hands and selected a place several yards away from Dan. He lay on his side pecking at the base of the seam and making a narrow cut under the coal, "dressing" it so as to loosen it from between roof and floor.

Dan paused for a moment, saying, "We'll get plenty of coal ready Glyn, it may be some time before the haulier comes. What's up, I wonder? There must be something wrong out there for him to be so late."

Glyn only nodded a reply for he had not yet recovered from the deep sleep. Some moments later he mumbled, "There must be something wrong Dan. The haulier's never been as late as this for a long time. We'll be late going home again. It'll be one great rush and late home!"

Dan did not answer but continued to release coal which he threw, with a short handled shovel, several feet back towards the road-head. After some time had elapsed, and the face was packed with cut coal, the man stopped working and crawled out of the face, stood up at the road-head and gazed down the dark road, listening for the sound of the haulier's horse and empty tram. He heard nothing except a rock squeeze and the scuffle of rats. He shook his head and grumbled. Time was precious and it was ticking away — time that couldn't be made up.

"What the hell's up down there!" he muttered to himself. He turned to the coal face and called out to Glyn. "There's not much else we can do now Glyn; no point in getting anymore coal ready. Bring the tools out."

Glyn gathered the tools together and dragged them out of the face and laid them against a dry wall.

"We've got enough ready for another two trams Dan. If he doesn't come soon we'll be late going out. What's wrong out there?"

Dan stroked his face with his large, bony hand and gazed down the black road, hoping the haulier's light would appear.

"Let's take a stroll as far as the double-parting boy," Dan said, "there's nothing more we can do here."

They unhooked their lamps from timber lids and went along the road. Near the end of the road they saw a light coming towards them. It was one of the hauliers. When he got close enough, Dan spoke to him.

"Where the hell have you been Jo! We're a tram adrift!"

Jo was a short, thickset man with a large bald head on which was a skull-cap caked hard with roof droppings. He was an excitable man who used his hands whenever he talked.

"It's Sam the pony, I knew it would happen again one of these days . . . I knew it!"

He wrung his hands, breathed short, quick breaths and looked up at Dan, pathetically.

"What's happened then?" asked Dan. "Come on out with it."

"He's pulled a tram over Charlie, a muck tram . . . O, he's in a hell of a state is Charlie! Give us a hand to unload the tram!"

Jo turned and made for the heading. Dan and the boy followed behind.

"I knew it would happen see," continued Jo. "I knew it. They shouldn't have given a horse like Sam to a collier to drive. When there's a haulier absent they should never give a horse like Sam to a collier!"

"Of course," said Dan, "but you know how things are down here; consideration's unknown."

"O hell, O hell!" muttered Jo as they approached a group of lights on the heading. When they arrived at the derailed tram three colliers were unloading rock from it quickly, and carefully. Unshackled from the tram, and standing several yards away in the dark, was the pony Sam, steaming, and shaking his head to disturb the flies. The section of the road was narrow and at a gradient, with water trickling down the smooth, rock sides. Under the front axle of the tram lay Charlie the collier; the axle was across his chest.

A bad spot here for pushing sprags into the front wheels, thought Dan. He could see that Charlie had been putting sprags into the front wheels and the pony had pulled the tram forward and trapped him.

The men continued to unload the tram, carrying the rocks to a place several yards away where there was room to build a wall at the side of the rails. There was great urgency in their movements; large pieces of rock were handled with ease.

"He put the sprags in at the wrong place see," muttered Jo. "I told him to change them in a wide place. You can't trust a pony like Sam in a narrow place like this. O hell! O hell!"

Jo hissed and wrung his hands as he thought of Charlie's pain; turning his back on the group he muttered to himself. He could not bring himself to watch them working. When sufficient rock had been unloaded from the tram they lifted the front end and Charlie was dragged away. The district official arrived and looked at Charlie, shining his lamp into his face. He looked up and saw Glyn who had pushed to the front to get a closer look at the unconscious man.

"Send that boy back to his road Dan," ordered the official.

Dan put his hand on the boy's shoulder, saying, "Put the tools on the bar Glyn and lock it, then get dressed and wait for me in the road. I'll be with you in a couple of minutes."

The boy went back to his road. Normally he would have been relieved to find there wasn't any more work to be done, but what he had just seen took away the relief and made him feel nervous and sick. He wondered how Charlie was. He remembered Charlie had volunteered to drive Sam that morning at the lamp-station. The tram was heavy . . . a muck tram . . . full of rock . . . three times the weight of coal. He thought of Charlie's pain and the stone stillness of his face under the light of the official's lamp.

He quickly gathered the tools together and threaded them on to a steel bar, locked them, then dressed. He took a drink of water from his bottle and emptied away what was left, then he walked back towards the heading. At the end of his road he looked towards the place where the accident had occurred. The lights had disappeared and there was no sound. The pony, Sam, stood in silence in the darkness of the heading. The boy lifted up his lamp and saw the pony steaming in the middle of the road. He went to the pony.

"You're really in trouble Sam," said the boy, stroking the pony's neck. "Why didn't you wait for a minute? Why did you pull on like that? You should be more careful with a collier behind you Sam."

The boy turned the horse around and took him back to his road, turned him again and backed him into the mouth of the road. He enjoyed handling the pony and imitating the horse-jargon used by the hauliers. The pony obeyed his commands, moving gently and quietly.

At the bottom of the heading the boy noticed several lights bobbing about, which made him wonder what was happening. He looked in the other direction towards the face of the heading, for there too were several lights, indicating some activity. The pony scraped his foot on the ground and shook himself to disturb the flies that had gathered on his warm skin. The boy took out his tommy-box and fingered out a sandwich which he gave to the pony who ate it quickly and began to nose in the boy's pockets for more.

"Get away" said the boy, "there's no more there, take your head away."

The boy, beginning to feel cold, drew out a scarf from an inside pocket of his jacket and wrapped it around his neck. He hitched his lamp on his belt and stretched his arms over the pony's back and felt the warmth of the steaming skin. He leaned his full weight on the pony and closed his eyes. The pony stood quite still, only twitching its rump skin to disturb the flies. From the heading came the sounds of men. The boy listened as they approached.

"Where the hell is he?" came a voice out of the dark. "He was standing in the heading when I left."

"Perhaps he knows we're after him, " said another voice.

"He can't have disappeared; a horse doesn't wander in the dark, that's for sure," said the first man.

The boy smiled at the men's concern.

"He can't have got far anyway. He's around here somewhere, must be," said the first man. He came to the mouth of the road and shone his lamp on to the pony and the boy.

"He's up here," shouted the man, "with Glyn."

The boy took his arms off the pony's back as the others came to the mouth of the road. One of them, a huge man with a beard and tobacco stained lips, looked at the pony.

"Don't go near him boy," said the bearded man, "he's a bad 'un — a killer!"

"He's all right," said the boy. "He's quiet with me here. I led him up the heading, turned him, and backed him into our road . . . he's not bad."

"We'll give him all right!" barked the bearded man, gripping Sam's bit-straps. "Come on, get up there!" commanded the man. The horse walked forward behind the man and disappeared into the darkness of the heading.

"Keep that boy in the road Dan," said the official.

"Have you locked the tools Glyn?" asked Dan.

"Yes, they're all safe," answered the boy. "What's happening Dan?"

Dan didn't answer. The others waited in silence just inside the mouth of the road, fingering their hair nervously and occasionally looking up and down the heading.

"What's happening?" asked the boy. "What's everybody up to? Can't we go home now Dan?"

"No, not yet, we'll only be held up. They're taking Charlie out so we'd better hang on here for a while."

"How's Charlie?" asked the boy.

"He's a gonna," said one of the men.

"Is he dead then?"

"Yes," said the man, "he's dead all right."

"Dead . . . that's terrible!" the boy said.

"Go back and get my jacket and shirt," Dan said, "and see that the tram is safely spragged."

The boy hurried into the road and collected the jacket and shirt and checked the tram. He knew there was something going on and he was curious to find out what it was. He almost ran back to the mouth of the road and handed the clothes to Dan.

A voice, loud and clear, came from the face of the heading. "Keep . . . clear . . . down . . . there!"

The men stepped further back into the road. Dan caught the boy by the arm and gently motioned him back a few yards, then he quickly put on his shirt and jacket.

"What's happening!" asked the boy. "Tell me Dan, what's happening!"

There was a sound of rushing air and the rumbling of a tram. The boy watched, breathlessly. The men were silent, listening and watching, their bodies tense. The rumbling grew louder and suddenly a pony and tram flashed past the road down into the darkness of the heading.

"That was Sam, wasn't it?" the boy asked.

They didn't answer his question but scrambled out to the heading and stood staring into the darkness after the pony and tram. The rumbling sound died away and there was a sudden crash and a rush of cold air followed by a silence.

"You've killed him, you bastards!" shouted the boy. "You've killed him, you've killed him . . ."

"He killed Charlie didn't he?" said one of the men, "and that other chap not so long ago."

"It wasn't Sam's fault, it wasn't Sam's fault!" the boy shouted. "He shouldn't have had a collier to drive him . . . it wasn't his fault!"

He left the group of men and rushed down the heading. When he got to the bottom the horse was lying crushed against the stout posts which had been placed firmly across the mouth of the heading. The tram of muck had spilled over him.

"You've killed him, you've killed him!" he shouted back at the men.

He scrambled over the rubble and laid his hand on the horse's head. Then he began clearing away the rocks which were strewn over the animal's body.

"Sam! Sam!" he muttered, struggling to tumble the larger rocks away from the pony.

The bearded man came out of the darkness and lifted him away from the dead horse.

"You've killed him, you've killed him!" shouted the boy, struggling to free himself from the man's powerful hands.

The man pulled the boy around to face him. "Don't take it hard son. This is the second man he's had since he's been down this pit."

The boy relaxed in the man's grip, scared by the power of the hands on his slim shoulders.

"It's for the good of us all see," the bearded man went on, releasing him, and putting his arm around the boy's shoulders. "He couldn't be trusted. He killed two men. You'll feel better about it in the morning."

The boy cried in the bearded man's arms as the others removed the posts and rocks to make a way through.

Terraced Houses, Abertridwr — Lyndon Richards

Rebel's Progress

Tom Earley

When idle in a poor Welsh mining valley,
Dissatisfied with two pounds five a week,
I got invited to a Marxist rally
And found to my amazement I could speak.

I soon could spout about the proletariat,
The bourgeoisie and strikes and lockouts too,
Could run an AGM or commissariat
As well as boss-class secretaries do.

At first I joined Aneurin Bevan's party
But soon got disillusioned with all that.
Joined Harry Pollitt and became a commy.
They turned down all my pacifism flat.

The hungry thirties found me hunger marching
To squat with Hannington inside the Ritz.
Then PPU. For just this I'd been searching
Before the war and long before the blitz.

I liked the people in the Peace Pledge meeting
But found that they were holier than me
So marched with Collins and quite soon was greeting
My former comrades in the CND.

To sit with Russell next became my hobby,
Vanessa Redgrave's fame I hoped to share.
Got thrown around in Whitehall by a bobby
And then a broken arm in Grosvenor Square.

So now I'll leave the politics to others
And not be an outsider any more.
I'll go back to the valley, to my mother's,
And never set my foot outside the door.

Except to go to chapel on Bryn Sion
And maybe join the Cwmbach male voice choir,
I'll sit at home and watch the television
And talk about the rugby by the fire.

The Drop-out

Alun Richards

It was nobody's fault, only circumstance's. You bring a girl up and she chooses wrongly, and that is that. Other people, as she said at first, made mistakes or were forced to change their minds and she was by no means unique. There was nothing special about her at all. Heavens above, why did everybody think she was worth staring at? Well, let them stare if they liked. And let them talk too, about the little matter of the ring — that was how she described it — let them gossip all they liked.

Mavis Thomas — she hated the name, but there it was, her name, a common one — was the second daughter of a colliery fireman who had suffered an injury in the pit and sunk his compensation money into a back street sweetshop, one of those front parlour businesses that break the uniform grey monotony of the South Wales streets. He had prospered by his standards and the family were what might be called very lower middle class. That is to say, they ran to a new second-hand car every five years and were the first in the street to have a fully automatic washing machine with spin dryer. They had also recently acquired a caravan near the coast where they spent week-ends when the father could be persuaded to leave the shop.

There were four of them altogether; Mavis's father, Walter Thomas, his wife, Mair, and the eldest daughter Pamela who was married to a television production assistant and lived in London. Both girls had been trained as shorthand typists and Pamela had met her husband at the BBC where she was employed. Her husband was regarded locally as a bit of a catch and during the time of Mavis's trouble — for that was how people described it — it was widely reported that the elder sister had spiked Ronnie's guns. Ronnie was Mavis's affianced and people who saw the two of them together were in no doubt that they made a perfect couple. What Ronnie lacked in social cachet — he was an electrician in a steel works — he made up for, not only by his good looks, but by his prowess as a rugby footballer. He was a fast-moving and powerful lock forward, a Welsh trialist, and had acted as reserve for the Welsh team in Paris on the occasion of their last defeat.

And here again, the miners who visited the shop said, life was a cow when you came to think of it — if Ronnie'd been capped at the time — if they'd let him have a go at the French, well, it was bound to have made a difference.

"Bound to have!" one said adamantly, "I mean, he've got a shove on him like a young bull. Let him loose in Paris, she'd have been delighted to have got him back at all!"

But Mavis hated the local humour, saw nothing at all amusing in their interminable jesting. She had taken pains to eliminate all traces of her Welsh accent, and had, until that happening with the ring, been keen to correct Ronnie's speech which smacked too much of the streets for her liking.

There was an incident when they were alone together in the caravan.

"Oh, come on, Mave . . ."

"No. Stop!"

"Stop? I can't bloody stop. One look at you lying there, and I'm like a hot frog in a big drought!"

She frowned. She knew that in its way, this contrived metaphor was intended as a compliment. But the sound of his voice when he made remarks of this kind in the local idiom went through her. She knew all about the difficulties which face engaged couples, and if he but knew, she had made up her mind in that direction without much uneasiness. But when he spoke to her in this way, as if she were a workmate, or some hanger-on in a rugby club dressing-room, it was demeaning and she felt it as a personal affront.

But he was very attractive. Apart from his considerable physique, he was — as everybody said — such a nice chap. His face was humorous, big-jawed and open, with quizzical blue eyes and a mop of curly black hair which he cut short in the season. He was also popular and generous, but most important of all, there was no doubt of his attraction, and when he first held her in his arms, she experienced such a thrill of passion that it quite unnerved her. They were a careful, thrifty family, not given to extremes, and while her father still had the blunt directness of the colliery, theirs was not a household in which they really talked to each other. "Don't," her father had said when she started to go out with boys. "Be careful," her mother advised. "Make sure," Pamela said, but really, Mavis felt this was not half the problem it was cracked up to be. What did unnerve her more was the way she could be this close to Ronnie — they were in their swimming costumes in the bunk of the caravan on a warm August night — and yet feel her composure and her desire shattered by one such remark.

"Oh," she said. "Very funny. I suppose you rehearsed that to repeat to the boys?"

Hurt, he grunted and turned over on his elbow so that no part of his body touched hers.

"No, of course I won't. What d'you think I am?"

That was the trouble. What did she think he was?

She had all summer to find out. In London, when they went to stay in her sister's flat, they were a great success. She had certainly never looked better. She was quite tall, dark and full bosomed with high cheekbones which gave her that slightly gipsyish look which Welsh girls sometimes have. She wore her hair in a high bun and did not say much, sitting rather aloofly in the parties her sister gave, causing everyone to look at her and one or two to think of trying their luck. But Ronnie, massively handsome in Club blazer and full of Welsh anecdotes, and more important, a fist that would have felled anyone in the room, stopped the more ambitious. They looked a happy couple and were much admired; although later, much later, she thought idly of one or two of the television men who had eyed her in that unmistakable way. Pity, she said to herself then.

It was a glorious but curious summer. They had a week in London and a week touring Cornwall on Ronnie's scooter. Pamela liked Ronnie. He was simple, good-humoured, and correctly respectful to her own husband who had just moved from Schools Broadcasts to Current Affairs. She gave Mavis to understand that she knew what it was like to be engaged. She quite understood the tensions, she said, but while they were up in Town – she'd got quite sophisticated – they could use the flat as they liked.

"You mean. . ." Mavis began, but she was cut short.

"Well, you're virtually engaged, aren't you?"

"Did you and Colin?" Mavis asked coolly.

Pamela, who was five years older, smiled condescendingly and went on filing her nails. "People are rather more sophisticated up here. I mean, it's not like being violated under a coal truck, is it?"

Mavis felt snubbed. It was not that she thought, What if mother could hear us? Both parents were so far removed from the world of the children that they were scarcely considered in important matters of any kind. They lived, bound to the shop, like little folk figures in a home produced Welsh drama. "Don't! Be Careful! Think ahead!" The admonitions of the past fell about the daughters' ears like dead weights. They were certainly no help to Mavis now.

"Oh, well," she said to herself. "I suppose, if I must, I must."

But when the moment came, her casualness deserted her. Although she acquiesced, she realized to her horror that there was some withdrawn part of her that coldly stood outside herself and she was afraid. She was not tearful with virginal apprehension, or even more sophisticatedly, a little put out by his roughness. She was suddenly quite aloof and unfeeling. She thought him — her betrothed — a fool.

"Oh, Mavis. . . Oh, honey. . . Come on. . ."

No word escaped her lips — there was nothing she dared say — but afterwards, lying there uncomfortably in her single bed, his huge frame inert beside her, she took stock of herself. She was quite tearless and unmoved. There was a physical discomfort she had not expected, but it was not her body that objected — she was healthy and strong — but as the seconds ticked by, she felt a sadness that was quite new to her. She was not shocked, nor indeed did she feel any of the things she expected to — neither guilt nor fear. "I'll be careful," he'd panted, but instead, in that moment, it was as if a blanket of disillusion had descended. Now there were no more mysteries. For all his size and charm, he was a child, a sullen, fumbling schoolboy and he did not need her except to use her to satisfy his own opinion of himself.

"How was that?" he asked. "Okay?"

God, if she told him, told anybody for that matter! She did not answer him and she had a sudden bitter feeling of intense hatred. They told you nothing — parents, teachers, the world in general and the Welsh in particular. If there was some cinematic close-up of them now, naked in each other's arms, her bruised nipple enmeshed in the prickly hair of his bronzed chest, there would be exultation, admiration, lust, even envy, on the part of the voyeurs. But their nakedness, the very position, was a grotesque lie. She had never felt so alone, or so miserable and utterly wretched.

"It takes a bit of time," he whispered in her ear.

She could tell he was sleepy and gulped her answer to the dark. "Of course." But how the hell did he know anyway?

"I mean . . ."

"I know what you mean." But she thought; Ugh! Was everything so squalid, so pathetic, so demeaning, so infinitely beneath all her ambitions?

But she was not unkind. She sensed his embarrassment and concern for her. Of course, everybody had difficulties. She knew that from the magazines and her mother had given her a copy of *Getting Married*, although she took care to keep it out of her father's sight. But this was the least of it. She had a suspicion that nothing begins or ends with the sex act and worse, an apprehension that they had come all this way only to find out they had nothing to say to each other. She gave a tremor as she felt his hand upon her breast.

"Oh, I love you," he said. "Honest."

Before she knew what was happening, she was crying. She could not stop herself. It was so sad and she hated herself for her detachment. He might have been some loveless waif of the streets washed up into her arms, she was that sorry for him. Poor wretch.

He held her tightly.

"I'm clumsy."

"No! Not at all."

"Well, I . . ."

"Forget it."

"Oh, I'm a bastard," he said guiltily.

But his remorse invoked her sadness all the more. There was nothing she could do for him; nothing. Until this moment, she had worn him as she might a dress, a decorative figure that she was glad to have on display beside her. That was the terrible thing. For five months they'd gone out and she was delighted by everything about him except his jokes. People envied her. Her parents took it for granted that they would be married. So did her sister. Even now her sister expected them to be locked in an embrace and there would be sly looks in the morning. And now here she was, beginning to shiver, bored with her nakedness and quite separate from him and everybody else. What next? What now? What to tell him?

"I want you to wear the ring in the morning," he said suddenly. "I've got it in my blazer. It's the one you looked at. I was going to keep it until Cornwall. But I want you to have it now. Please. . ."

"Oh. . ." She'd looked at it, it was true, but she hadn't tried it on.

"Will you wear it?"

"Now?"

"No, in the morning. Better not try it on now. It's sure not to fit and I don't want to spoil tonight," he said grinning.

"Oh, I see."

"Will you wear it? I'm not good enough for you really. I don't speak so nice as you do."

"Never mind!" It was out of her mouth before she could stop herself, but she thought, Christ, she was too bloody charitable!

"Oh, Mave, you'll wear it?"

She felt the tears well again. "Yes," she said. She had to. She was a coward too when it came to it. And so old fashioned. No good moaning about her parents. They were all cowards and it was catching. Her parents never said anything about anything and her sister made these blasé jokes. "Don't! Be careful! Be sure!" They were all tarred with the same brush when the crisis points of living were reached. Their inarticulacy was an assumed thing, a protestation against the hazards of living and they made themselves gnomic so as not to take any risks. Her parents must have begun their entry into the trance-like state by not telling things and she was like them. She could tell him nothing. She felt more miserable than ever. "Yes, I'll wear it, and I'm sure it fits."

"Oh, Mave'," he said. He squeezed her hand. "I think you're great, aye."

But after the bleak moments which followed what she was to call all her life, her grubby initiation, everything seemed to go more smoothly for them. Life is not all it seems in borrowed beds, and in the next week, they caught the beginning of a heat wave and toasted themselves on the Cornish beaches. Once again, his attractiveness reasserted itself and she was conscious of the envious looks of other girls. Temporarily, what she spoke of in her mind as the sex thing, was shelved by an arrangement they came to, and it was simply good to be alive on those simmering beaches. They had come on holiday, she meant to have a holiday and she did. She was not the self-pitying sort. They were young, healthy, with money in their pockets, and the sun shone.

And thus, they returned from their holiday bronzed and refreshed, and that far off London happening and the little embarrassment in the caravan, were as remote in her mind now as coins tossed into the bottom of the sea. What were two small specks amongst all that water?

But winter came and all its South Wales trappings. Ronnie now became serious about himself and his football, and she soon learned that, as he was such a strong prospect for the national team, there were certain things with which she was expected to put up. She had virtually to give up seeing him for three nights of the week when he was training, and on Saturdays when he was playing away, he could not be expected to see her at all. For home fixtures, he made a concession, but then he was not free of his commitments until it was too late to go to any of the places she preferred. The cinema was out and the dances that she would have liked were not in reach because he would not leave the boys in time to travel. Instead, they went to a local hop with the rest of the team, and this she did not like because some part of her remained outside the beery conviviality that always sickened her on these occasions.

It was the supreme irony that she was not in the least interested in what everyone else was so passionately concerned with — Ronnie's inclusion in the Welsh team. Other girls, and sometimes it seemed to her, half the town, stopped him on the streets to express their hopes, but she regarded them all with an amused smile. It was only a game that men played until they grew up and she could not understand what all the fuss was about. Ronnie tried to explain but the problem defeated him. If the Welsh language was threatened, the coal industry staggering under-manned on its last legs, the Methodist chapels boarded up, the town *Fifteen* still retained the élan of old. They were a supreme in-group and the kudos that attached to them was in no way diminished by the ravages of the sixties. Pop groups and cinema stars were outside figures, but the *Fifteen,* the boys, as Ronnie called them, remained local property and were regarded with tribal affection. And this in turn, had its effect on the boys. Inclusion in the Welsh team, the *XV,* was almost regarded as if it were enough to set up a man for life without ever working again! It was very perplexing.

But Mavis could have put up with it all were it not for the effect it had on Ronnie, the endless training, the moodiness that came upon him when he had a bad game and sometimes lasted for days — it all seemed to her to be futile. It was bad enough expecting her to be bear-hugged and pawed by his jocose friends in the Saturday night dances. He had a habit of expecting her to dance with all of them and passed her around as if she were already his property. But there were even worse things and one of them led directly to the little matter of the ring.

One night they went in a borrowed car to a seaside hotel where she was at last to be granted her wish that they attend a dinner dance with no one else present. She was by this time sick of the gregariousness of the football season. The smell of linament, the bawdy songs, and incredibly — the maudlin Revivalist hymns that arose from the steaming showers while she waited outside for him on training night after training night had finally caused her to put her foot down. She felt, as others had felt in turn before her when confronted with the unshakeable selfishness of most male institutions, that she could stand it no longer. She must get away. And she must get him away. And to her joy, he acquiesced. But no sooner had he said yes, than he added the information that there was a big game coming up and he needed a change to take his mind off it.

"To take your mind off it?"

"Well, it's a Welsh trial. You know what they are — everybody out to impress and some out to get you."

"Oh, Ronnie . . ."

He did not notice her face; "Do me good to think of something else for a bit."

"And me?" her voice was small and peevish.

102

"Ah," he gave her a broad grin, "you know what the season is. I've got to get in this year. If it's not this year, it'll be never."

"So?" she was openly sneering in one sense, and yet another part of her cried out for some attention. She had a sudden insight of how other people would have regarded the situation, especially those new friends of her sister's. How they would have been amused! An extra-marital rugby liaison . . . You can have the Pill but not the ball. Everything that hurt the Welsh most was intensely amusing in London. Perhaps that was why nothing ever got done properly in Wales. Where the power was, people only laughed. From the Metropolitan point of view, they were all freaks! "So?" she repeated. "Suppose you never get a cap?"

He glowered sulkily at this blasphemy. "I told you we'll go," he said. "There's no need to be a cow about it."

That adjective! Oh, she could have given him the ring back there and then.

But he caught her arm; "You know it means everything to me. Don't look like that, it's a great thing. Representing the country doesn't happen every day, and it doesn't happen to many people. It's special. It's an honour. If we have kids, well, isn't it something that their father has a cap?"

She hesitated. She was not a bit moved yet she knew that her mother would have been in tears. That was how they all were, prostrate at the mention of such ambitions. But it was always the idea of representing something, not doing anything — that was the secondary thing. The myth always preceded the action, then choked it. Still, it was his obsession. "If you want to," she said, assuming a loyalty she did not feel. She was frightened about that. The whole winter had been a little unreal but now the feeling of that lonely moment in the bedroom returned. She had to pretend to a feeling and she sensed the danger. They were too young to start doing that.

On the way to the coast in the car, she was very quiet. They were engaged to be married and she did not treat it lightly but everything that seemed to be happening to them was so trivial and insignificant. Perhaps she was too much of a realist. One thought stuck persistently in her mind. They were only going out on the town now because ground frost had caused a rugby match to be cancelled. "Oh, Christ!" she said to herself with a flippancy that was shocking. She swore a lot lately. "Offside again." She was a rugby drop-out.

In this mood, she got down from the car and accompanied Ronnie into the dining-room. There was no preparation for the last straw of the season. No sooner had they sat down at the table and she had begun to admire Ronnie in his dinner jacket, than she saw him stiffen and a glazed look come into his eyes as he glanced through the alcove into the cocktail bar. He flushed with nervous excitement and gave a little gasp.

"What is it?" she said.

"There," he whispered in a hoarse voice.

"What?"

"Over there, holding the Pimms."

"I can't see anything." She liked to appear quite composed in public places and she felt his agitation did not become her.

"Mr Rockford Williams," he said.

She did not understand. Was it his employer? Both she and her sister had had to fend off theirs. Thoughts of rape and lechery arrived at the office party with the predictability of Christmas cards.

"The Big Five," he said deferentially. "I'll have to go and speak to him."

"Speak to him? We've only just come. Big Five?" she was in a daze. But she realized what he meant. The Big Five selected the team. They were national football selectors and if you had Ronnie's ambition, they were very important. But suddenly her disappointment welled and she was so sick of it all that she knew she was going to make an issue of it. It was as if a veil of unreason descended, blanketing her good nature and changing the expression on her face. All right, she said to herself; it seemed trivial and funny and fey and Welsh, but God she was not going to go through with the farce for one minute longer. She could just imagine how he would behave in the bar in front of the personage. He would be an owned man. And she wanted someone who owned himself. She knew — ah, she really knew! — just how he would be — humble, well intentioned, sincere and keen, a good boy, a nice boy, such a lovely chap, not drinking very much in the season, thank you — training! But she would let him choose now and see what he was made of.

"If you don't stop that gawking I'll get up and walk out

now,'' she said. She was quite amazed at the sound of her own voice, it was hard and cold, a determination in it that did not sound like her at all.

"What?" he could not believe his ears. He blinked at her, a blush spreading from under his chin as his mouth gaped open with incredulity.

She did not hesitate for a second. "For one night I want to think of something else."

"But . . ."

"It's no good. I'm not going to talk to him. I am not!" she raised her voice, at the same time experiencing a unique thrill as she caught sight of people at another table turning to look at them. Now she was becoming a celebrity!

He sunk his chin into his chest and growled across the table at her. "I'll go on my bloody own then," he said thickly. His ears were scarlet.

"Well, if you do, you won't find me here when you come back."

He gasped and half stood up, hesitated for a minute undecidedly so that she thought he was going to hit her. But then he drew himself up firmly and moved the chair, bending over to hiss in her ear.

"I'll give you one more chance," he said shrilly.

But she could not contain herself, nor hide the look of contempt on her face. How could he behave like this? "Oh, balls!" she said, spitting out the unaccustomed word and in the same instant knowing that he would repeat it to his mother that night.

He gasped, turned as if struck, and then lurched beetroot-faced into the cocktail bar where he at once addressed the notability with a cringing, "Good evening, Mr Rockford Williams" that she heard from the table. She was on her feet in a flash, moving in a flurry of temper, stripping the ring off as she went. Then she paused in the alcove and threw it with a quick deft flick of the wrist so that it landed noiselessly on the carpeted floor between the two of them.

"Keep your bloody ring," she said. In temper, her accent returned and while she was speaking she was aware that she was shrieking like a market fishwife. "Keep your bloody ring. Convert that if you fancy it more."

They looked at it and at her, Mr Rockford Williams, a paunchy ex-athlete with an inflamed broken nose, boggling behind business lenses, and Ronnie, almost hysterical with embarrassment and fury.

"She . . ." Ronnie began to say, but she did not wait. She bounded out of the hotel, her steel-tipped heels chattering under the maxi that she had bought unnoticed for the occasion. She was soon at the bus stop where she waited a full forty minutes without even bothering to wonder if he would search for her.

And he did not. It was in fact a month later when seated on the railway station, London-bound with all her luggage packed, that she saw him again. His photograph was in all the papers. He had achieved his ambition, had acquitted himself like a man in that direction, and when she saw him, he was off to Scotland to represent her there. He did not leave the main party, merely waved sheepishly and then got into their reserved compartment with all the elderly hangers-on.

Some of the boys who knew the story chaffed him good-naturedly on the train. He did not say much. It was all so embarrassing.

"Well, I don't know," he said eventually. He'd been told she was moving to London. "I bet she'll bloody eat them up there."

Had she heard him, she would probably have thought it the most juvenile remark he could have made. Without affectation, she felt she was above him and all of them now. She was — was she not? — growing up. "Don't! Be careful! Make sure!" What phrases to start your life at twenty-one! She had only one phrase for her future. "Find out!" And she added another with a touch of devilry that delighted her. "Find out — and winner take all!"

She repeated it to herself as they started on the hymn singing further down the train. They began with *Cwm Rhondda,* the favourite of the crowds.

> "Death of deaths
> And hell's destruction . . ."

But she only wondered idly, how much he'd got back on the ring.

Synopsis of the Great Welsh Novel
Harri Webb

Dai K lives at the end of a valley. One is not quite sure
Whether it has been drowned or not. His Mam
Loves him too much and his Dada drinks.
As for his girlfriend Blodwen she's pregnant. So
Are all the other girls in the village — there's been a
                              Revival.
After a performance of Elijah, the mad preacher
Davies the Doom has burnt the chapel down.
One Saturday night after the dance at the Con Club,
With the Free Wales Army up to no good in the back lanes,
A stranger comes to the village; he is, of course,
God, the well known television personality. He succeeds
In confusing the issue, whatever it is, and departs
On the last train before the line is closed.
The colliery blows up, there is a financial scandal
Involving all the most respected citizens; the Choir
Wins at the National. It is all seen, naturally,
Through the eyes of a sensitive boy who never grows up.
The men emigrate to America, Cardiff and the moon. The
                              girls
Find rich and foolish English husbands. Only daft Ianto
Is left to recite the Complete Works of Sir Lewis Morris
To puzzled sheep, before throwing himself over
The edge of the abandoned quarry. One is not quite sure
Whether it is fiction or not.

Old Tips

Jean Earle

Over the years, a tip would take on time's finish,
A greening over —
Seen from far off, a patina
As on bronze memorials. It was a feature
Of place and weather: one of the marks of home
To my springloaded people.

Autumn in the allotments. Sunlit on high,
The town shadowed, all its pits asleep.
Sometimes the cows off a neglected farm
Would stray across a very old tip —
Lie around on the strange, wispy grass,
Comforting their udders.
For the tips breathed out a warm greenish smoke
After rain, suggesting thin volcanic pastures.

Some were known as wicked, secreting runnels
Of black treacle-death. They swallowed houses
Helpless at their feet.
But most were friendly.
We children ran out of school,
Visiting the one that loomed
Close to our playground.
Shouting, we stumbled towards the top
And saw a dandelion burning in the grit
And that abandoned crane pointing
To the annual sea.

from Before the Crying Ends

John L. Hughes

There being nothing special much around this town. Not like London nor Paris nor Rome nor Lisbon nor Washington. Not like Cardiff nor Tenby nor Bangor nor plenty of towns you can see anywhere.

No one particular item making you sit up sudden like you never believed what you saw first time off. Not a single special thing for making passing (on to God knows where) strangers remember where they been. No special beauty. No special ugliness. No sudden visions. And no sudden blindness as ever they (them passing strangers) could recall.

Nothing special much around this town for filling empty exiled nights and minds with nostalgia nor things hard to forget a hundred a thousand a hundred thousand miles away. Nothing memorable you understand. No one peculiar thing them passing eyes could retain for ever. No wide gasping geographical statement marked deep across the landscape making them (them passing strangers) whisper all holy:

Only God could have done that.

Now tell me there is no God.

God been poking his fingers up this place.

God definitely done that mountain (or that valley or that cliff or that forest or that sky).

Even the name of this place is forgettable. Pontypridd. A shambles of mystic Welshness. Pontypridd. Something to do with a bridge (there is a bridge). Pontypridd. Something to do with the earth (black stuff). Who could remember such a name? Who could care?

There being nothing special much around this town. Nothing at all. Except perhaps the river. Maybe just that.

The River Taff. Swilling down from Merthyr same as some kind of whip. Dirty candle-coloured by day down through Aberdare Mountain Ash Abercynon and Cilfynydd in a torrent. In a welter of torrents. Grunting sucking lashing whirlpools blackened through by mining trash and coal no man could burn.

109

Twisting fast down deep inside the guts of Pontypridd. Towards Cardiff. Carrying things. Always carrying things.

Dead terrier. Four headless chickens. Five loaves (from Wonderloaf) and two fish (from Plowman's) floating in circles amid surface scum just off that Marks and Spencer back wall. Two mangled oil cans from Texaco (by way of Halfords) and one sodden *Western Mail* hanging same as nests on the pea-shooter beds fringed haphazard around Ynysangharad Park. And a bucket. And a bugle. And a birthday card. And a trouser leg with the turn-up down. And a boy and his ferret hunting for rats.

Found a bike down there once.

Only needed a chain.

Found a chain down there once.

Only needed a bike.

And in flood that river is mighty. A frightening thing. Unstoppable (if ever man had a mind). Creaking heavy against them quaking banks where houses stand. And people stand. Staring. Up at the rain. Down at the river. Across at each other. Wondering. With tomboys chucking stones snick snick into the grey flow. And today it is raining as last night it rained and the day before. And the night before that day. For this town is Pontypridd. Where they know all about rain.

And it was raining when you got born. And it will be raining when you die. If you die in Pontypridd.

And mister I can tell you for nothing as how when that day comes you will definitely have enough on your plate working your dead mouth on a fiddle into Heaven never mind that hissing rain.

With thoughts like that definitely giving you the willies now and again seeing as how you are not ready for no bloody drop this fair side of three score years and ten. With a stack of functioning left for doing inside your skull not to mention all through your medium rare skin. Leaving them passing strangers to keep on passing by this forgettable place in a gust of wind and rain. On towards London or Paris or Rome or Lisbon or Washington or Cardiff or Tenby or Bangor or anywhere else. For this town is Pontypridd where the gods brought your soul at the beginning of time. And nailed it to the wall.

Local Boy Makes Good

Harri Webb

When Christ was born on Dowlais Top
The ironworks were all on stop,
The money wasn't coming in,
But there was no room at the Half Moon Inn.

The shepherds came from Twyn y Waun
And three kings by the Merthyr and Brecon line,
The Star shone over the Beacons' ridge
And the angels sang by Rhymney Bridge.

When Christ turned water into stout
A lot of people were most put out
And wrote cross letters to the paper
Protesting at such a wicked caper.

When Christ fed the unemployed
The authorities were most annoyed;
He hasn't gone through the proper channels,
Said the public men on the boards and panels.

When Christ walked upon Swansea Bay
The people looked the other way
And murmured "This is not at all
The sort of thing that suits Porthcawl."

When Christ preached the sermon on Kilvey Hill
He'd have dropped dead if looks could kill
And as they listened to the Beatitudes
They sniffed with scorn and muttered Platitudes!

When Christ was hanged in Cardiff jail
Good riddance said the *Western Mail*,
But, daro, weren't all their faces red
When he came to judge the quick and the dead.

Elegy for Wiffin

Meic Stephens

You lived by us in Fothergill Street, but
my mother always kept me from playing with you.
You were sure to come to a bad end, she said,
with your name in The Pontypridd Observer.
For that, I wanted to be your butty, Wiffin,

especially when, on summer evenings,
the railway-siding's gorse was set alight
and the neighbours put the likely blame on you;
watching the fire-brigade from my window,
I took your part against their brazen tongues.

Why did you go and die like that?
Mitching from school, it was a wet Friday,
we balanced like two small Blondins
along the girders at Glyn-tâf weir — until you fell,
Wiffin, into the river and drowned.

What the police expected to discover
by pumping the industrial water away,
I was too brave to ask. Under the arc-lamps
the reeking mud yielded nothing but its own depths.
I could have told them you weren't there

for during the next few weeks, you and I
played together in all the prohibited places:
you showed me how to prise lead from factory roofs
and smash the sodium lights on Llantwit Road.
I felt your presence in my delinquent arm.

It wasn't until your withered body
fouled the cooling-tower's nets at Upper Boat,
two miles down the valley, I had to admit
that it was all over between us: from then on
I would have to watch my step, like a good boy.

Home Comforts, besides the Convenience all Round

Ron Berry

Boys being what they helplessly are, we imagined roles for Mildred Taylor, the lavendered reality of our carnal budding. We cast her in situations of erotic fancy with Pip Pearce, who taught General Science. Tunneling libidos like tormented moles, we laid small, hot bets, simpling her whole life and times. Mildred Taylor *was* beautiful, utterly, earnestly lovely with a crystaline soprano voice that trembled her soft white throat. Entering our classroom for singing practice, she personified the opposite of utility female, of bosom and loins. Our Miss Taylor shone. She was rare, ethereal, too perfect. Her dainty hands and feet were mesmeric flickerings, ineffectual perhaps . . . how were we to know? She wore flowered frocks, her dark hair cherubim-curled, scented for rousing puberal madness. Pretty girls worshipped her, plain girls envied her, sullen girls brewed malice, muttered liturgies of disaster.

One afternoon she fainted at the end of the last line of *Flow gently, sweet Afton*, while leaning over Albie Charles, who sabotaged every singing lesson.

"I tickled her bum," Albie said.

Pip Pearce carried her out to the staff room. Tall, tweedy, smarmy, treacherous as migraine, wavy-haired, hard-eyed, you'd see him flashing his choppers at Miss Taylor, his rugger shoulders immaculate for symmetry and poise. They were lovers, we were dead certain, fast couplers on a par with any two outside the dull hell of compulsory education.

I whispered to Albie, "Shurrup, keep your trap shut."

"Guh, 'fraid," he said.

Then Pip Pearce charged in again. "You! Get out. Wait for me in the cloakroom."

Therefore Albie did it, brought on the swoon, otherwise Pip wouldn't have swung at him, sick-squealing, "Dirty little

113

swine, you dirty little swine,'' his horizontal karate chops landing on Albie's ribs.

Albie went home with a letter from the headmaster.

Next morning at eleven o'clock, Albie's old lady and his brother came strolling across the school yard. "Righto, Mam, leave him to me," Albie's brother said, swaying slow, Pip Pearce dipping the same way, soul-trapped as a rabbit, into a fast left hook.

Miss Taylor wept, secretly sobbed all day, her violet eyes grieving, flinching from Albie like you see in dingy old paintings of spectators at the Crucifixion.

And now only last Whitsun I met Albie Charles for the first time in seventeen years. He jumped out from the yellow Landrover, yelling, "Hey, for God's sake!" a cigar aimed at my mouth, his big, meaty hand dragging me into the Queen's Hotel.

I said, "Great to see you, Albie. Right in the money by the looks of it."

"Two large whiskies," he said to the barmaid.

She dibbled her lips with her tongue as if she'd flog him two of anything.

"Money," he said, quietly incisive, "boy, last year we cleared five thou. I've just pulled a contract for laying two miles of kerb. That's what I'm in, asphalting and laying kerbs."

"Where?" I said.

"Anywhere, anywhere at all." The barmaid counted his change. "Ta. Say, what are you having?"

"Um, drop of gin. Ever so kind of you, Mr. . .?"

"Albert Charles, love, Albie Charles, born and bred in this little town. What's the tariff here in the Queen's? See, I'm around for a few months, swanning to and from Bristol till next winter. Look, bring the manager, okay?"

"Here's to days gone by," I said.

He sniffed his whisky, muttering, "Thank Christ."

I said, "This particular couple of miles, where are they?"

"Your new council estate, the lot, plus the run out to the motor-way."

"Pondorosa," I said. "We call Hafod Estate Pondorosa, from that crap show on telly."

He grinned fatly complacent. "Things don't change much

over the years. They build a new housing estate, but Hafod isn't good enough, the locals tab another name on it."

"Married yet?" I asked.

"Hah, awkward bastard," he jeered genially, his finger and thumb doing a slow-motion castanet for the barmaid. "Same again, my dear. Keep the supply handy."

I left him chatting up the manager.

Less than a minute after I closed my front door, Hester reached for her cracked glacé handbag. "If you can guzzle whisky when there's five weeks rent owing, I can borrow a few bob to visit my father. I'm entitled to! Good-bye!"

She slammed the door.

"Stay with your old man, don't bother to come back," I said, not even hoping any more because after seven begrudged years of quibbling you suspend all hope, quit everything except the habit of tit for tat. In marrying Hester I took on one of those daunting Electra girls. Tomorrow, I thought, I'll see Albie out on Hafod Estate. He's successful. Something might rub off.

But I dithered, avoided the issue until Saturday, riding a cheap conviction that Albie's firm wouldn't be working a six day week. I could have seen him any night in the Queen's; pride's a canker when you can't jingle two silver coins in your pocket.

My wife said, "Albie Charles, ugh, him, dragged up he was."

"You haven't set eyes on Albie since we left school," I said.

She sneered, "I'm worried sick."

You fish-blooded nun, I thought, before asking, "Remember the time he tickled Mildred Taylor in singing practice?"

Hester stalled, snorting endless resentment, her down-cast mouth clamped on it.

Husk-head, all mine under licence.

"See you around dinner-time," I said.

"Scrag-end stew!" she protested. "I don't know, we're existing worse than refugees. This isn't what I was brought up to, never on your life."

"Your generous old man might throw us some surplus caviare," I said.

It's a slanting climb up to Hafod Estate, the higher Clearway edged into ferny hillside, travelling a shallow curve around the mountain. After dark, traffic headlights veer away, reversing to red tail lights as vehicles take the steep S bend which clears the summit. I walked in mid-morning sunshine, the Estate glittering. Saturday kiddies and summery women were out on the trot, husbands potching in their first-crop gardens, cheerfully automaton breadmen, milkmen, insurance men, H.P. collectors, and dogs. Neurotic dogs everywhere, barking off the tops of breeze-block walls. Typical Glamorgan mountain clay gardens, ochrous, cold quilt covering the best steam coal in the world. Idling up through the Estate, I heard her greeting before I saw Miss Taylor, beckoning dignified as royalty on the new front lawn of her three roomed bungalow. Not all that old, really; she'd be thirty-sevenish, wrapped in a flowery frock as always, exquisitely Dresden, her complexion dreamed out of the beauty closet of her sincere soul.

"Well indeed, how pleasant," she cooed. "Another of my pupils. Come inside, I have a surprise for you."

Albie was studying the *Sporting Life.* He wore a poncy dressing gown and red leather slippers. A red polka dotted cravat poutered beneath his blunt chin. And bald, Albie, smooth-white bald as a bladder of lard. He ripped the *Sporting Life* in half, humphed disgust as he heeled himself away from Miss Taylor's dinky little writing bureau. "Out of bounds, boy," he said. "I thought you lived the other end of town."

"He does, Albert," her gently levering arms bringing us together. "Now, shake hands like gentlemen."

"We've already met. Listen, Millie, how about some coffee?" he said, stuffing the torn racing paper into his pocket. "Heavy night last night. I had my C. and P. experts from Bristol." Albie exaggerated the shakes of his right hand. "Look at that, can't steady my fingers. Eyeballs like sheep's currants in the snow, can't see properly. Fetch the coffee, Mill, ah, if you don't mind?" He went back to the bureau, sheafed some loose pages, puffs and grunts escaping from his tight mouth.

She twitched between pleasure and guilt, creases serpenting the bland forehead below her dark hair. "I understood it was a formal dinner, token of goodwill in your business. Surely?" She touched his cheek with the tips of her fingers. "All right, I'll make the coffee."

116

He grinned, watching her tripping out of the room. "Some bird. She sat up most of the night waiting for me."

"What's going on then?" I said.

"Going on! I'm just the paying guest. We bumped into each other a fortnight ago. See, I'm criticising the service in the Queen's, so Mildred makes the offer. Full room and board. Suits me, home comforts, besides the convenience all round." Albie palmed his stomach. "I'm heading for alcoholism, don't fancy it either, seen too many clever bastards hit the bottle and land in the shit." He worried through the loose pages on Miss Taylor's bureau. "Trouble is, boy, her ideas are different from mine. She knows nothing about pressure."

I said, "How about fixing me up with a job ?"

A shaft of sunlight swooped across his baldness, like a straightened aureola. "My pleasure. You'll be labouring. It's piece-work, good money once you harden to the graft. Another thing, don't lose any time or you'll be up the road. Can't afford sentiment on this contract. It's all tight, real tight."

"Start Monday morning?" I said.

Albie nodded, sunshine starring the buffed ivory of his dome. Miss Taylor's curtains pinkened the room. It was peaceful, charcoal drawings of prancing stallions hanging each side of the window, two tall bookcases full of book club best sellers, a round dining table, flower-print cushions ribboned to Queen Anne style chairs, embroidered cushions correctly scattered on the settee, below a flying wedge of terracotta mallards geometrically plaqued to the wall. A fan of pink-stained teazel stalks sprayed upwards inside the fire-place.

When she brought the coffee I remembered my drab, anguished Hester, her wearing rancour, her wifely uselessness.

Albie shook out three pills from a plastic phial. "Revivers," he explained.

"Do be careful, Albert. One hears so much about harmful drugs."

"Never panic, I'm no gutless fool," he said, swilling them down with coffee. There was a stoniness on him, a kind of bloodless indifference. "Pip Pearce still on the staff?" he said.

She stared at nothing, the whites of her eyes not quite so moon-glowing. "Phillip Pearce? Well, you know, he couldn't

117

settle down. Phillip transferred to a small country school, in
Devon I believe. Yes, north Devon. His parents left soon
afterwards. Mm, how long ago it seems.''

Albie said, ''That's life. Water under the bridge. That's the
way it is. He wasn't a bad fella, old Pip Pearce.''

''He dealt you a real lamping one time,'' I said, stupidly
forgetting Miss Taylor serenely perched between us at the
table.

Albie scowled, left his chair, focussed the same scowl on his
business papers. ''Right,'' he said. ''Eight o'clock Monday
morning. Bring your insurance card.''

''See you,'' I said. ''Thanks for the coffee, Miss Taylor.''

Her chin trembled innocent delight, the way she sang for us
when we were kids, pouring her soprano into *Flow gently, sweet
Afton*.

Later, over the scrag-end stew, I told Hester about Albie
lodging with Miss Taylor. She wasn't interested. Hester
nagged, threatened to stock her wardrobe instead of paying our
rent debt. They'd perished, all her school-time memories were
squashed under the weight of her father. He ruined Hester's
childhood. Ruined her, his lorn child. My stultified wife.

Summer spent itself, contrary as usual in up-and-down
Glam., but autumn brought golden, windless weather, sapling
poplars planted to beautify Hafod Estate taking on rusty tints,
decay creeping slow from the highest tracts of hillside bracken.
Albie's firm employed two gangs of men. The top gang were
kerb-laying down a slip road from the Clearway; the second gang
worked on Hafod Estate. Houses were still going up. Slum
clearance families swarmed in. More dogs, cats, plastic
footballs, airguns, pigeons, napkins, transistors galore. When
the children returned to school after their long holiday, Hafod
Estate folded quiet. I worked with Albie's top gang, always
behind the concrete mixer, consequence of rowing with the
ganger. This charming navvy despised slum clearance families.
Naturally enough they had a sad percentage of crocks and
cripples among them: bad chests, stomach ulcers, rheums,
skewed genes, game legs, weak minds, burnt nerves. He'd
taken a strong dose of white-man's toxin, this cranky avant

garde navvy, so I shovelled into the mixer and humped kerb-stones.

For weeks on end we saw Albie belting along the slip road in his yellow Landrover. Then came the first hard night frosts. Both gangs were concentrated on Hafod Estate to finish off the contract.

Saturday evening, November the fifth (the date guaranteed to stick), a huge staked Guy flared paraffin flames in the backyard next to our house. Lower down the terrace some lads were launching sky rockets, tangentially though, instead of vertically, aiming them at next door's Guy. Speaking truthfully, I'm partial to a stint of chaos. Chaos ferments the tired old dough of homo erectus, keeps it on the rise.

Hester called from the kitchen window. "S'long, I'm away now. I'll be home tomorrow night."

"Enjoy yourself," I said. She spends well-nigh every weekend with her father. Military Medalist from Tobruk, her widower dad, ex-sergeant major to boot. Fine hero. Messed-up his only daughter.

The lads from lower down began tossing jackie-jumpers and bangers when Albie arrived. It was like a tiny edition of warfare, these fizzers suddenly banging off, taming the autumn stars to tenth rate.

"You should know why I'm here," he said, lighting his cigar from the glowing remains of a firework. "Job's almost finished, but listen, boy, if you come to Bristol with me I'll make you up, put you in charge of a small gang. All the extras. I can't be fairer."

I said, "Much obliged. I'll stick it out here. We may come to terms some day, Hester and myself I mean."

"We've all got problems," he said. "Right then, c'mon, let's sink a couple in the Queen's. I want you to do me a personal favour."

Miss Taylor was waiting for us in the lounge bar, tenterhooked as a maiden aunt behind a tall orange juice, too much of her real age showing, pitiful, a loose lemon yellow coat hiding her secret belly. On the second round of drinks I called Albie across to the counter. "You didn't tell me she was pregnant," I said.

The barmaid had survived, ceased to appreciate him. She

signalled a friendly little flutter of the fingers to Miss Taylor, who strained a return smile that left her defenceless. Mildred Taylor looked stricken, wrecked on biological ignorance.

Albie brought his mouth down to my eye level. "Here's what I'm asking you to do for me. Monday morning after I pull out, call in the bungalow. I'll arrange it with my foreman. Make her understand I won't be coming back. Two reasons. First, there's my wife and three daughters in Bristol. Second, we're starting a long contract out Keynsham way. Means I've got to be on the spot. Wait, take it easy, boy, take it easy. Listen, I'm paying for everything, see, everything. After the nipper comes along she'll collect a nice lump sum through the post."

I said, "Why bring me into this?" the barmaid's ears inching closer to clinch what she probably suspected. "You can't expect me, Albie," I said, "to take on the responsibility."

"Christ," he vowed, "al'right, I'll tell her." His fist softly bumped the counter. "Know what her trouble was? She'd never sampled it before. Never. Hard to credit, that, couldn't believe it myself at first. I reckon she's cried every night for two months, give or take a few here and there. By the Jesus, she's like a drain, cry-cry-cry night after night."

Fireworks were cracking off outside the Queen's and somebody lobbed a Thunderflash into the public bar. Women screamed as expected. It was a provocative atmosphere.

"Your wife," I said, "what's she like?"

"One of the very best." He emptied his glass. "If she comes to hear about Mildred, huh, I'd sooner settle for a bed of stingie nettles."

"Afraid of your wife?" I said.

"No-no. . ."

"Yes-yes," I said.

The barmaid served him a double whisky. Albie sniffed it, emptied the glass, bought himself another beer, grunted a kind of private righteousness against destiny, and, "Lead the way," he said.

Miss Taylor nervously plucked her curly-whiffed hair, the delicate ovals of her nostrils red raw as the inflamed poop-holes of sickly babies. I noticed some of her eyelashes were stuck together, as occurs when stye pus crystalises during sleep. Poor Miss Taylor, she looked hag-ridden. Contractor Albie, he pulled thuggish faces at a fresh cigar, his match-hand glinting a thick gold ring on the statutory bloody finger, Miss Taylor's face emptying, dredged beyond hysteria.

"That," she quavered, "means you are a married man."

"Speaks for itself. Aah, listen, Millie, I fully intended informing you about my wife. . ."

"Take a walk," I said. "Wait for us in the lobby."

Albie shrugged like a bit-part actor, swerved up from his chair and strolled out, grossly immune in his Dak business suit and dove grey hat.

Miss Taylor winced herself smaller inside the lemon yellow coat. Time spayed out of whack while she struggled to find the child-like composure of her youth. She smiled. "I'm not a vindictive person. It isn't my nature."

"What will you do, Miss Taylor?" I said.

"I am quite capable of looking after myself. Circumstances being what they are, I must make plans for the future." The smile sputtered out as faint remorse. "As for Albert Charles, may he rot in his own wickedness."

"Buy yourself a wedding ring," I suggested. "Nobody'll be any the wiser, I mean we can place one of those In Memoriam notices in the local paper, bury Albie somewhere the other side of Severn Bridge, bury him forever. More important, Miss Taylor, consider the financial aspect. The man's afraid of his wife. He's harmless. We've got him over a barrel."

Panning her violet eyes, she murmured, "Aren't you a cunning devil."

"Hester trained me," I said.

She stretched almost a pretty smile. "Strange, the girl was absolutely tone deaf."

I said, "Aye, true, true. Ready now, Miss Taylor?"

"Perfectly ready."

"All that remains to be cleared up," I said, "is how much he's prepared to pay. We'll have it in writing, my signature as witness, just in case."

Giggling relief, dimples plucking each side of her mouth, she confessed softly, "Phoo, I'm glad it's all over. Tonight I shall sleep in peace."

Here's proof, I thought. Innocence conquers experience.

Standing on the pavement outside the Queen's, she ignored

Albie, her small hand cheekily wriggling the funny bone of my elbow. "You must bring Hester to tea next Sunday evening. Promise."

"Bank on it," I said. "In the meantime I'll discuss details with Albie. We'll draw up a statement."

Tinkling like a girl, she hurried across the road to a Hafod Estate bus.

Albie trod on the butt of his cigar. "What's all this about a statement, boy?"

"Safety precaution, Albie, confidential, as regards your wife."

"How much?" he said.

"She insists on bringing in a lawyer, blood tests, evidence from her diary, loss of income in due course. . ."

He kicked the flattened cigar. "I'll talk her out of it. Few hundred made out to the kid, that's my limit."

I said, "Three thou as a starter – I'm quoting Miss Taylor – then thirty-three and a third per cent until the child is sixteen."

Adrenalin cued a flood of spittle to his mouth. He couldn't speak.

"You're still young," I said. "Only my age. Too young for a heart attack. You might as well hear the facts first as last."

Then, "Bitch," he snarled, lowered his head and booted the front tyre of his Landrover like a lunatic. Strong man temporarily out of his mind. A spectacle hard to forget.

We buried him fictiously a month later, via notices in two newspapers. Mildred's son was born under Aries, the true amalgam of his mother and Albie. Fixing fate for a plump, gurgling baby happens to be the Holy Ghost's prerogative, but as the child's god-father I predict wolverine tenacity tempered by angelic sweetness. I prophesy total commitment balanced by loving kindness. He'll be unique, a phenomenon out of ancient Cymru.

Dic Dywyll

Mike Jenkins

I have banished God
further than the Antipodes
since my so-called accident.
He was the owner
of those mills of death,
his manager the old Cholera.
The preaching of Cheapjack remedies:
holding up heaven as a cure.

They took my eyes
and struck them
into cannon-balls.
My mask and its perpetual night
is known to the pit-ponies.

Crossing the Iron Bridge
I hear the river's voice
bring tune to my ballads,
the hooves of canal-horses
count beats and pauses come
as I breathe the welcome wind
from the west and eventual sea.

Night arrives and they all
share my mask: punchy drunkards,
rousing rebels and laughing ones
who sup to conquer daytime.

My daughter is the blackbird
giving flames to the begging hearth
of our basement with her song;
and I am the owl, I turn
to face their sufferings,

call them out to chase away
the chimneys' shadows. Masters
I magic to mice
under the death's-head moon.

Note:— Dic Dywyll ('Dick Dark') was a balladeer in 19th century
Merthyr Tydfil. He was blinded while working at Crawshay's
ironworks.

Neighbours

Mike Jenkins

Yesterday, the children made the street
into a stadium, their cat
a docile audience. As they cheered
a score, it seemed there was a camera
in the sky to record their elation.

Men polished cars, like soldiers
getting ready for an inspection.
Women, of course, were banished
from daylight: the smells of roasts merging
like the car-wash channels joining.

Today, two horses trespass over boundaries
of content; barebacked, as if they'd just
thrown off the saddle of some film.
They hoof up lawns — brown patches like tea stains.
They nudge open gates with a tutored nose.

A woman in an apron tries to sweep away
the stallion, his penis wagging back at her broom.
I swop smiles with an Indian woman, door to door.
These neighbours bring us out from our burrows —
the stampede of light watering our eyes.

Tondu — Pandora Allin

from The Visitor's Book

John Davies

1.   Just where along the line did this voice start
    chirping *cheerio* and *chap*, my language
    hopping the frontier? Things fell apart,

      the sentry cannot hold. Distant, he will keep
      barking 'Where d'you think you are, boy? On stage?
      Back of the gwt!' My cover, see, isn't deep:

      my ear/year/here sound suspiciously the same.
      Should I say 'I'll do it *now*', don't bank on it.
      And, upstarts, some new words seem assumed names:

      brouhaha sounds like the Tory Hunt tearing fox
      -gloves. *Rugger* too. I can't say *Dammit*
      or ride phrases trotting on strong fetlocks.

      These days, language slouching through me lame
      from the States is — well, a whole new ballgame.

6.   The t.v. set, stirring itself, confides
    in my father in Welsh. Bored, I can see
    outside the steelworks signal in the sky
    to streets speaking pure industry.

      His first language I did not inherit,
      a stream my father casually diverted
      to Cymmer clean past us all. Brisk shifts
      of my mother's tongue worked in my head.

      My wife and daughter speak it, strumming
      on green places, a running water-beat
      beyond me. But though I've picked up some
      of the words they do not sound like mine.
      It is like hearing what might have been;
      pointless to mourn that far-off rippling shine.

8.   'Why can't poems be clearer? This one
    of yours—' Even now my mother makes me jump.
    That afternoon, by car, we tracked the sunlight
    to hazed terraces where Cymmer tumbled
    half in the flustered river, where the house
    once ours blinked its bay-window modestly.

    While she went visiting, I could make out
    the road's allusions to stone, obscure trees,
    up where it pencilled lines about the heat
    on grass. Still I'm unsure just how far
    to follow it. We talked of the street
    later, people we'd known way back. And briefly
    they shimmered in the windscreen, stars
    almost there as I took the sky's veiled slack.

10.   A sonnet's no shape for the geography
    or life round here, you say: too cool, too neat
    by half for these valleys' buzz and heat.
    Hell, you've been reading again, Welsh Disney
    stories full of Dai Oddball in a whirr
    clean out of his mine, a hwyl-happy freak
    down the Con Club proving that plotless weeks
    don't happen. I've had him up to here.

    As for the landscape, this stretch of valley
    narrowed my focus fast. See how the slopes rhyme
    mirror-like to the Afan's tidy rhythm?
    How everything runs down in symmetry?

    No. Well . . . I've been away too long
    to catch the place's rough and ready song.

Rough Justice

Graham Allen

It began with the new rugby ball, George's birthday present.

We ran the ball in the fields above his parents' small-holding. Below us the lower Swansea valley, the rows of terrace houses with vee-shaped roofs, regular and glinting like the teeth of a saw. And on the bottom of the valley, all the different works, with long sheds and a few flashing sky-light windows — black and white like dominoes in the evening.

At first we were afraid to kick the ball. We wiped it clean on our coat-sleeves every time we dropped it. I liked smelling the bright leather and lifting the ball close to my face until my teeth were gently against it.

When the time came to run home alone, I clutched an imaginary ball to my middle, leaping the rain pools that shone quiet on the stony path, crunching over the packed cinders that filled in some of the puddles outside a couple of small-holdings—running, running fast through the flap of wind, side-stepping, swerving between the pools until I seemed to hand and lean on the wind itself, sleeked into it, breathing in laughs.

"Mam? Mam?" I ran through the house calling, even tapped on the lavatory door out in the backyard. Then I knew she'd be in the front bedroom keeping one of those vigils where she'd have me sit with her and wait up for my father's late return from the pub. And I preferred the bitter decorum of such vigils to going to bed. It was worse there waiting for the shouting downstairs to stop, growing anxious in the silences and ready to believe anything had happened, so that my ears, one moment pressed shut into the pillow and bed-clothes to escape the shouting, now strained breath held, to hear scufflings, scrapings.

She was sitting in the window and ignored my greeting. I told her about George's new football. The wind in my ears and my breathlessness gave way to the curt click of knitting needles. "Show me your shoes," she said, "if you please." I lifted a foot to the dim light that seemed to stagnate around the white lace

129

curtain hanging over the lower half of the window. "Like cardboard," she said. Then she went on and inspected me thoroughly. She felt across my shoulders and down my back for dampness until her hands seemed awkwardly idle so that she flicked at my hair. But she didn't pick up her knitting again. She got up, saying, "Come on then, in the bath with you. The fire's been drawing all evening. Not that he'll bath now." And then she added, "The waster might drown!"

Later that night, I woke blinking into the kitchen light. I could smell my father's beery stubble and the greased clothes of the works. He knocked the chair as he tried to wrap me in a tipsy smother. But it was my mother's curses that really brought me to. These were terrible both to herself and to me, for she was a chapel-going woman. Indeed the curses were his, she took them to use against him, so much did his look of dirt and drink and shabby weakness incense and infect her.

When he fell asleep in his chair she left me with him. "That's your father," she said, and turned her back on the two of us, going wearily out of the kitchen and along the passage to the stairs. So she abandoned me to the sleeping figure and left me stranded in the lighted kitchen, watching my father twitch in his sleep, hearing the steady tick of the clock without listening, but most of all giving her time to climb the stairs before I could creep up to bed into the ease of the darkness.

Next day, a Saturday shopping afternoon in Swansea, she bought me a football. It was a gift out of the blue, no worry, no bargaining, no saving. She reclaimed me utterly saying she was mother and father both in our family. The manager patted my head and smiled: "That's the genuine article, that is. You're a lucky boy." His words — more than hers — quickened within me a fury against my father.

Back home, we walked up to the park where I could show off to her my kicking and passing. But often she looked away up valley and beyond the stacks and the glinting tips pricked by shafts of sunlight like beetles on a pin to the clear, cold line of the mountains. There were a few trees, bare and forked like children's slings on the sky-line, quite anonymous.

"Catch!" I yelled, and threw the ball to wake her up. Then we lobbed it to each other until she started to run so quickly and unexpectedly that I scuttled off behind her in surprised delight.

She stopped, forgot the ball, and caught me up in full run, swinging me about her, and laughing.

"We must go though," she said, and went back for the ball. I jumped along at her side, full of admiration. "You can run fast, really Mam!"

Now she held the football between her hands, looking first at it and then at me. She seemed to gather and bunch herself in. Her eyebrows were taut and straight and her eyes had settled on the ball. She spoke evenly without a trace of laughter and gathered me easily into her plans, trusted but negligible.

"We'll see how far his money goes now then," she said. "Won't we just!"

I never had the strength to disown that ball, though many times I tried to kick it out of sight and lose it.

One evening she made me sit and wait while she completed her chores with grim thoroughness. Then she did his jobs with an abrupt, restrained fury of gesture — full of reprimand should I fidget around her while she chopped sticks, got in the coal, or attempted to mend shoes in front of the hearth. "This is what he thinks of you," she said, "you really count for him." And all the time — I could see it even then — what she said to me, she meant for herself. She stopped working and held me at arm's length. "There, there" she made much of me. There was nothing like that pity for convincing me of my father's contempt.

Later that night she roused me from bed and got me downstairs to act as witness. For my father was asleep in the chair. He was not expensively drunk, for he became light-headed on the smell he'd sniff in any accidental draught squeezed out by the opening and shutting of a bar door. It was his apartness she couldn't stand, his sleeping isolation. Above all, the way his dapper ease and insouciance seemed blurred, weak. She tried hard to preserve all her puritan fight in our corner of industrial South Wales, but weakness frightened her. She glimpsed her own frailty in the downfall of others. So she could be very cruel. It was she who always punished me, never my father. She kept a yellow switch behind the pantry door.

"Look your fill," she directed me. "Here's something to remember." The mere sight of the man's small figure crumpling into sleep, and still in work-clothes, urged her to

131

rush water from the kettle onto the fire. And as the coals smoked wetly, she fell scuffling upon him, using his curses again and all the obscenities she always tried so hard never to hear.

I can't remember exactly when I thrust my fingers into the smouldering fire. Or why. Only that the pain expressed my feelings as they fought. My involvement and my uselessness found an intense relief.

And all was fixed on that moment when my father struck her. It was a quick blow on the face, but hard and deliberate. It parted, it stopped them, it was final as the blood flowed.

They must have turned to me almost immediately, for I was screaming by now. Yet I've never forgotten my father's blow. It wasn't at all retaliatory. It was a spontaneous response not to any hurt of his own but to some sense of justice she'd infringed falling upon him as he slept.

Savage it was, but not without a bold rightness after so many words, after my incidents and all the matter of the football.

I never forgot his roused indignation, though it was just that one blow I ever saw. Then he proved bewildered himself, and almost apologetic. So that when the doctor arrived to treat my burned hand I lied.

"How in Heaven's name did you manage this, young 'un," He spoke very genially and didn't seem to want an answer. Perhaps he'd grasped something of the quarrel between my parents. At least he asked me about my Mother's cut mouth.

"My Father hit her," I said. But I couldn't go on to tell him just how it had been. That was the first time I couldn't trust a grown-up with the truth.

"He beats her," I said.

"No, surely not?"

"Yes," I said. "Yes."

Abercynon

John Fairfax

At the face of Abercynon the cutting screw
Chews out a bite 2ft 3inches deep by 153ft long.

In the lampbeam the coalface shimmers
Black that holds in it a memory of sun and rain.

Short hydraulic props probe flat iron plates
Against torn scars. And behind the prop the roof falls.

Coal and slate-dust clams mouth and nose and pores
To conceal the low tunnel and blot out thought.

The black dust breaks lampbeam, seeps into eye socket
Rasps on the tongue and is sour bile in the throat.

The coalface screams. A stream of water splashes
On tungsten cutters ripping out the narrow seam.

Crouched with more than a thousand feet on his shoulder
The miner holds a prop handle, pushes and turns to move
        the prop.

The iron plate grinds into the gap left by the cutter
Metal and coal war while a man crouches between

Moving each prop down the cut-line, adjusting thin mesh
Between prop and roof; joining mesh plates with silver
        spring.

Abercynon gives up its coke coal foot by foot,
Tonne by tonne, to the bone and flesh of miners.

Each face is unthinkably sunk below layers of earth.
Black lives. Black silence punches the whistle out of a man.

Rhigos

Robert Minhinnick

The cannon-smoke rolling
Off the Beacons engulfs the car.
The violence is over
Yet a promise of lightning
With its cordite tang hangs over
The khaki drab of Hirwaun.

Above this mist they gaze
From the stacked flats:
Faces between the turrets,
Hands clenched without weapons.
The only armour here
Is isolation that toughens

The mind, hardens eyes
That stare from siege. I think
Of the people who live
On these battlements: old
Women white and frail as moths,
The men mulattoed by alcohol,

Their frustration which burnt
A hole in life itself burnt out.
Leaving nothing. And as we grind
Over the mountain gridiron
I know they are seeking us
And our movement's illusion

Of freedom, those old people
Standing at their balconies
In the fresh wind, yet

Seeing instead this prow
Of Glamorgan — the black
And naked Rhigos, a whalebacked

Massif that supports
Nothing of their life, that
Is no comfort, yet is the earth
To which they are fused —
Its cloud and violet skeins of light;
An unendurable rock.

Biographical Notes

SAM ADAMS: b.1934, Gilfach Goch. A former editor of *Poetry Wales* and of several anthologies, he is an H.M. Inspector of Schools. His collection of poetry *The Boy Inside* appeared in 1973.

GRAHAM ALLEN: b.1938, Swansea. He has published one poetry collection, *Out of the Dark* (1974), having concentrated since on prose writing. He is Vice-Warden of Coleg Harlech.

RON BERRY: b.1920, Blaenycwm. His novels and short stories evoke, often comically, the relative stability and prosperity of post-war life in the Rhondda Valley. A miner before he served during the War, his novels include *So Long, Hector Bebb* (1970).

ROY BURNETT: b.1929, Gelli. A businessman, his book of poems *Rhondda and the Collected Works of Dai Cottomy* was published in 1969.

A.J. CRONIN (1896-1981): b.Cardross, Dunbartonshire. After a medical career which included a period as a general practitioner in South Wales, he gave up medicine in 1930 with the success of his first novel, *Hatter's Castle* (1931). Some of his novels have made successful films and television serials.

BRYAN MARTIN DAVIES: b. 1933, Brynaman. A writer in Welsh he has won the National Eisteddfod crown twice. His poetry collection *Deuoliaethau* (1976) contains several poems dealing with the relationships between Welsh and English cultures.

JOHN DAVIES: b.1944, Port Talbot. Now an English teacher in Prestatyn, Clwyd he is the author of *At the Edge of Town* and *The Silence in the Park,* and editor of *Clwyd,* a similar anthology to *The Valleys.*

IDRIS DAVIES (1905-53): b.Rhymney. He worked as a miner for seven years then began to write poetry during a three-year period of unemployment from 1926, having been deeply affected by the General Strike and its consequences. His *Collected Poems* (1972) confirm his place as the foremost poet of the Valleys.

J. KITCHENER DAVIES (1905-52): b.Llwynpiod, Dyfed. Poet and playwright, a committed and politically active nationalist, his work (in Welsh) arose out of the Depression of the Thirties. Best-known perhaps is his radio poem *The Sound of the Wind that is Blowing,* composed on his death-bed.

RHYS DAVIES: b.1903, Clydach Vale. He went to London at the age of twenty, and after various jobs there devoted himself entirely to writing. A prolific novelist and writer of short stories, his *Collected Stories* appeared in 1955 and an autobiography during the late nineteen-sixties.

JEAN EARLE: b.1909. After leaving the Rhondda Valley when she was twenty-five and working for a time in various legal and diocesan offices, she now lives in Dyfed. Her poetry collection *A Trial of Strength* was published in 1980.

TOM EARLEY: b.1911, Aberpennar. An English teacher at a London grammar school for much of his life, his collection *The Sad Mountain* (1971) explores his roots in South Wales.

JOHN FAIRFAX: Poet and children's novelist, living in Berkshire. His poems include the poetry collection *Bone Harvest Done*. He was co-founder of the Arvon Foundation's creative writing courses.

JOHN L. HUGHES: b.1938, Pontypridd. His novels, including *Tom Jones Slept Here* (1971), are set firmly in the Valleys of recent times. A specialist in remedial education, he works in Bristol.

EMYR HUMPHREYS: b.1919, Prestatyn. Author of more than a dozen novels, including his latest *The Anchor Tree* (1981), he has won several major awards and prizes. He is also a critic and poet, his collection *Ancestor Worship* appearing in 1971.

MIKE JENKINS: b.1953, Aberystwyth. In the past a teacher in Northern Ireland and West Germany he now works in Merthyr Tydfil. Also a short story writer, his poetry collections include *The Common Land* and *Empire of Smoke*.

D. GWENALLT JONES (1899-1968): b.Allt-wen, Pontardawe. He was imprisoned as a conscientious objector during the War. A Marxist early on, a nationalist later, in time he joined the Welsh Presbyterian Church and his mature poetry is forcefully religious. His last collection of poetry was *Y Coed* (1969).

GLYN JONES: b.1905, Merthyr Tydfil. During a long and active literary career, he has published novels, collections of short stories and poems, and an influential study of Welsh writing in English, *The Dragon Has Two Tongues* (1968).

GWYN JONES: b.1907, Blackwood. Professor of English at Cardiff, he edited the *Welsh Review* (1939-49), translated *The Mabinogion* with Thomas Jones, and published several novels and collections of short stories. Recently he edited *The Oxford Book of Welsh Verse in English* (1977).

JACK JONES (1884-1970): b.Merthyr Tydfil. Novelist, playwright, propagandist, everything, he led a turbulent and full life. Starting work underground aged eight, he began to write only in 1926, literature and politics interweaving henceforth with the many other strands of his life. Of his eleven novels, best-known is *Rhondda Roundabout* (1934).

LEWIS JONES (1897-1939): b.Clydach Vale. His novels, which include *Cwmardy* (1937), arose out of his experiences both as a miner and an active Communist during the early part of the century.

ALUN LEWIS (1915-1944): b.Cwmaman. He was pre-eminently a writer of the Second World War − especially in those short stories and poems he wrote as an officer in India − as well as one of its victims. Like so many other writers, though, he was permanently influenced by the Depression. His work is well represented in *Alun Lewis: Selected Poetry and Prose* (1966).

SAUNDERS LEWIS: b.1893, Wallasey, Cheshire. Passionately committed to the cause of the Welsh language, a founder-member of Plaid Cymru, he was a writer of prophetic stature in several fields and one of the most influential figures in twentieth-century Wales. His many plays include *Cymru Fydd* (1967).

ROBERT MINHINNICK: b.1952, Neath. He has published several collections of poetry, including *Life Sentences* (1983), and won the Welsh Arts Council Literature Prize in 1980.

ROBERT MORGAN: b.1912, Aberdare. His twelve years as a miner in the Cynon Valley strongly influenced his subsequent work as poet, painter and writer of short stories. An autobiography, *My Lamp Still Burns,* appeared in 1981.

LESLIE NORRIS: b.1921, Merthyr Tydfil. He has recently been visiting Professor of Poetry at the Universities of Washington and Utah; among his seven books of poetry is *Mountain Polecats Pheasants* (1974) and he is also a critic and award-winning writer of short stories.

ALUN RICHARDS: b.1929, Pontypridd. The author of novels, plays and short stories − including those in *The Former Miss Merthyr Tydfil* (1976) − he has also written many television plays and adaptations.

MEIC STEPHENS: b.1938, Pontypridd. He founded the magazine *Poetry Wales* in 1965, later becoming Literature Director of the Welsh Arts Council. He has edited numerous books, including the *Writers of Wales* series, and a collection of poems *Exiles All* was published in 1973.

GWYN THOMAS (1913-1982): b.Cymmer, Porth. Most of his novels, plays and short stories wittily evoke life in the Rhondda during the Depression. In 1962 he gave up teaching to live by his writing and – as a noted raconteur – his work for radio and television. His *Selected Stories* were published in 1984 by the Poetry Wales Press.

JOHN TRIPP: b.1927, Bargoed. He worked as a journalist in London until 1968 and since returning to Wales has published poetry and short stories. His *Collected Poems* apppeared in 1978.

HARRI WEBB: b.1920, Swansea. He worked in publishing (including a period with the Druid Press, which first published R.S. Thomas) and public library service before becoming a full-time writer. A prominent member of Plaid Cymru, his collections of poetry include *The Green Desert* (1969).

VERNON WATKINS (1906-67): b.Maesteg. A close friend of Dylan Thomas, he lived most of his life in or near Swansea. His poetry, including *I that was born in Wales* (1976), earned him many literary prizes and awards, and he was also a noted translator. He was a poet of the inner life, writing little about matters of political and social concern.

ISLWYN WILLIAMS (1903-57). A writer of short stories, his work appeared frequently in *The Welsh Review* during the nineteen-forties and is also represented in the anthology *Welsh Short Stories* (1956).

Acknowledgements

'The Collier': © Gwen Watkins; originally published in *The Ballad of Mari Llwyd* (Faber & Faber).

Bidden to the Feast: © Jack Jones 1938; originally published by Hamish Hamilton Ltd.

'Rubaiyat': © Roy Burnett; originally published in *The Anglo-Welsh Review*.

'The Dead': © D. Gwenallt Jones; Welsh version originally published in *Eples* (Gwasg Gomer). Anthony Conran's translation: © Anthony Conran; originally published in *The Penguin Book of Welsh Verse*.

'The Public House': © Rhys Davies 1946; originally published in *The Trip to London* (Heinemann).

'The Mountain Over Aberdare': © Gweno Lewis; originally published in *Raiders' Dawn* (Allen & Unwin).

'Cadi Hughes': © Glyn Jones; originally published in *The Blue Bed* (Jonathan Cape Ltd.) published here by permission of Glyn Jones and Laurence Pollinger Ltd.

'The Sound of the Wind that is Blowing': © Mair Davies; first published in *Cerddi Hir* (Gwasg Gee). Joseph Clancy's translation © Joseph Clancy; first published in *The Oxford Book of Welsh Verse,* ed. Gwyn Jones (O.U.P.)

Times Like These: © Gwyn Jones; originally published by Victor Gollancz Ltd.

'The Deluge, 1939': © Saunders Lewis; originally published in *Byd y Betws* (Gwasg Gomer). Anthony Conran's translation: © Anthony Conran; first published in *The Penguin Book of Welsh Verse* (Penguin Books Ltd.).

We Live: © The Estate of Lewis Jones; first published by Lawrence & Wishart Ltd.

'Gwalia Deserta XV' and 'Gwalia Deserta XXVI': © Eben Morris published in *Gwalia Deserta* (J. M. Dent & Sons Ltd.).

'Little Fury': © Lyn Thomas; originally published in *Gazooka* (Victor Gollancz Ltd.).

'The Ballad of Billy Rose' and 'Barn Owl': © Leslie Norris; first published in *Finding Gold* and *Mountains Polecats Pheasants* (both Chatto & Windus).

The Citadel: © A.J.Cronin; originally published by Victor Gollancz Ltd.

'The Doctor': © John Tripp; originally published in *Collected Poems 1958-1978* (Christopher Davies Ltd.).

'Smells': © Islwyn Williams; first published in *The Welsh Review*.

'Mynydd Gilfach': © Sam Adams; originally published in *The Boy Inside* (Christopher Davies Ltd.).

The Best of Friends: © Emyr Humphreys; originally published by Hodder & Stoughton.

'Tairgwaith': © Bryan Martin Davies; originally published in *Poetry Wales*.

'In the Dark': © Robert Morgan; originally published in *Planet*.

'Rebel's Progress': © Tom Earley; originally published in *Welshman in Bloomsbury* (Outposts Publications).

'The Drop-out': © Alun Richards; originally published in *Dai Country* (Michael Joseph Ltd.).

'Synopsis of the Great Welsh Novel' and 'Local Boy Makes Good': © Harri Webb; originally published in *The Green Desert* (Gwasg Gomer).

'Old Tips': © Jean Earle; originally published in *The Anglo-Welsh Review*.

Before the Crying Ends: © John L. Hughes; originally published by The Bodley Head.

'Elegy for Wiffin': © Meic Stephens; originally published in *Poetry Wales*.

'Home Comforts, Besides the All Round Convenience': © Ron Berry; originally published in *Planet*.

'Dic Dywyll': © Mike Jenkins; published here for the first time.

'Neighbours': © Mike Jenkins; originally published in *Empire of Smoke* (Poetry Wales Press).

'The Visitor's Book': © John Davies; originally published in *Poetry Wales*.

'Rough Justice': © Graham Allen; originally published in *Planet*.

'Abercynon': © John Fairfax; originally published in *The Anglo-Welsh Review*.

'Rhigos': © Robert Minhinnick; originally published in *Native Ground* (Christopher Davies Ltd.).